D1291125

ADMINISTRATIVE AGENCY LITIGATION

ADMINISTRATIVE AGENCY LITIGATION

Christopher B. McNeil, JD, PhD

NATIONAL INSTITUTE FOR TRIAL ADVOCACY

© 2011 by the National Institute for Trial Advocacy

All rights reserved. No part of this work may be reproduced or transmitted in any form or by any means, electronic or mechanical, including photocopying and recording, or by any information storage or retrieval system without the prior written approval of the National Institute for Trial Advocacy unless such copying is expressly permitted by federal copyright law.

Address inquiries to:

Reprint Permission
National Institute for Trial Advocacy
1685 38th Street, Suite 200
Boulder, CO 80301
Phone: (800) 225-6482
Fax: (720) 890-7069
E-mail: permissions@nita.org

Library of Congress Cataloging-in-Publication Data
McNeil, Christopher B.
  Administrative agency litigation / Christopher B. McNeil.
      p. cm.
  Includes index.
  1. Administrative procedure--United States. I. Title.
  KF5407.M39 2011
  342.73'066--dc23
                                2011022121

ISBN 978-1-60156-144-2
FBA 1144

13 12 11 10   10 9 8 7 6 5 4 3 2 1

Printed in the United States of America

To Camille, Amanda, Caitlin, and Ian, with all my love.

CONTENTS

CHAPTER THREE: PREPARING YOUR CLIENT AND THE ALJ FOR AGENCY
FACT-FINDING

CHAPTER FOUR: PUBLIC RECORDS REQUESTS, IN CAMERA REVIEWS,
SUBPOENAS DUCES TECUM, AND OTHER ALTERNATIVES TO DISCOVERY

CHAPTER FIVE: RECOGNIZING THE LIMITS OF EVIDENTIARY HEARINGS BEFORE GOVERNMENT AGENCIES

CHAPTER SIX: BEST EVIDENTIARY PRACTICES FOR AGENCY LITIGATION

Chapter Seven: Collateral Challenges and the End-Run Around the Agency

Chapter Eight: Settlement Tools: Alternative Dispute Resolution, and the Threat of a Fee Award

Appendices

---

* Reprinted with permission. © National Conference of Commissioners on Uniform State Laws.

INTRODUCTION AND ACKNOWLEDGMENTS

Ronald Reagan used to say the three big lies of our time are "the check is in the mail," "I'll respect you in the morning," and "I'm from the government, and I'm here to help." Being the populist that he was, Reagan the candidate, and Reagan the President, knew we all harbor at least a little bit of dread when dealing with the government. Our collective experience when dealing with bureaucrats at all levels of government sometimes leaves a bit to be desired, especially when we hope to resolve a dispute where the government itself is a party.

At the same time, our collective experience over the past forty years has borne witness to an amazing expansion of governmental programs, created by our legislatures and carried out by our executive and administrative offices. We may not trust the government, we may grouse about its inefficiency, but again and again, we create administrative systems by which the government is expected to "be here to help."

I was fortunate, when at the University of Kansas School of Law, to take a course in administrative law from Professor Richard J. Pierce Jr. Professor Pierce let it be known that lawyers have a significant role in shaping the course of conduct between government and the governed. In particular, I learned how to link effective administrative governance with fundamental principles of fairness in the way our government carries out its responsibilities. The magic and meaning of "due process" is never so prominent in legal work as it is in the practice of administrative adjudication.

This book is designed to ease your transition to administrative practice. It's not a treatise—many excellent ones exist, including those written by Professor Pierce (which I highly recommend). It is, instead, a manual designed for use by persons with at least some legal training, including paralegals, students in clinical service, and nonlawyers working with or for government agencies. It was written as a guide to those who find themselves involved with governmental decision making, where the decision involves civil action by the government, affecting a property or liberty interest. The eight chapters that follow are intended as a roadmap to assist the reader in getting from point A to point C, without missing point B.5 or the hidden text at point C, footnote 2.

Experience drives most of what follows. Before becoming a federal administrative law judge, I spent eight years as an assistant attorney general advising state agencies and prosecuting occupational and licensing cases. This experience helped me to understand what motivates the people whose calling includes service in the executive branch of government. I found these people to be genuinely concerned about the policies under their jurisdiction. I also found them to be largely selfless and dedicated to performing in the public's best interest.

The experience also gave me the chance to litigate against some of the best litigators in the country. Make no mistake, one of the best features of working in a high-profile public office like that of the Ohio Attorney General is the opportunity to learn what it's like to get your clock cleaned by a seasoned litigator. The tricky thing is, however, that administrative litigation is significantly different from civil or criminal litigation. The purpose of the book is to identify those differences and explain how to adjust your approach to litigation to better suit agency adjudication.

I should acknowledge some measure of bias, based on experience. After serving as an assistant state attorney general, I spent fifteen years as an administrative adjudicator for various state agencies, including those agencies regulating doctors, nurses, engineers, surveyors, chemical dependency counselors, day care providers, Medicare providers, foster care providers, and others. My bias is this: I think if you're going to take it upon yourself to represent yourself or others in agency hearings, you pretty much have to learn the rules before your first contact with the agency. Legally trained representatives who come to a hearing without first learning about the process will almost certainly face a skeptical adjudicator. Even persons appearing without counsel have some duty to learn who bears what burdens in these cases. Follow the steps outlined in this book, and you'll avoid many of the pitfalls commonly seen in administrative litigation.

This book benefited from many sources. I want to acknowledge the debt I owe to the late John Hardwicke, who became Maryland's first Chief Administrative Law Judge. Judge Hardwicke was both mentor and friend for many years, and his unwavering devotion to due process and fair hearings is his eternal legacy. I also want to thank Judge William F. Dressel, president of the National Judicial College. The College, under Judge Dressel, has made outstanding progress in developing training programs to help administrative adjudicators understand and apply due process principles. In addition, I want to acknowledge the efforts of James T. Richardson, JD, PhD, head of the Grant Sawyer Center for Justice Studies and the Judicial Studies Program at the University of Nevada—Reno. Under Professor Richardson's guidance, the Judicial Studies Program has become a significant resource for judges of all stripes, who want to improve their understanding of due process and fairness in all forms of governmental adjudication.

I also want to recognize the support provided to me by Barry T. Simons, a member of the bar who practices in Laguna Beach, California. Barry is a founding member of the National College of DUI Defense, and is well versed in the administrative side of DUI prosecutions. I turned to Barry when I was researching perceptions of fairness in implied consent hearings, while working on my doctoral dissertation. Barry enthusiastically supported the research that supports the dissertation findings, encouraging administrative practitioners across the country to express their views about the fairness of those hearings. Much of what I have learned about the defense side of agency adjudication came from the responses given during this nationwide research.

The national survey conducted during my doctoral research and discussed in chapter six was supported by a grant from the National Science Foundation. The survey questions and the analysis of the responses appear in my book, *Perceptions of Fairness in State Administrative Agency Proceedings: Applying Theories of Procedural Justice to State Agency Hearings* (Lambert Academic Publishing 2009).

And last, while I currently serve as a federal administrative law judge, what follows in the next eight chapters draws primarily from my experiences prior to my entry into federal service in 2009, not from my work with the federal government. The views expressed in this presentation do not represent the views of the Social Security Administration or the United States Government. In writing this book, I have not been acting as an agent or representative of the Social Security Administration or the United States Government in this activity. There is no expressed or implied endorsement of the views or activities described herein by either the Social Security Administration or the United States.

Chris McNeil, JD, PhD

September 2010

CHAPTER ONE

UNDERSTANDING THE UNIQUE CHARACTERISTICS OF AN AGENCY-RUN HEARING

Topics in this chapter include:

- Practical Differences in Agency-Run Hearings
- Jurisdictional Differences Based on Time
- Differences in Access to Relevant Information
- How the Scope of the Hearing Makes a Difference
- Example—the Implied Consent Hearing
- Why Is an Agency Hearing This Case?
- How Do Agencies Control These Hearings?
- Consider Who Will Serve as the Adjudicator
- Find Out Who Will Represent the Government
- Differences in the Burdens of Proof
- The Role of Credibility Determinations
- Realities of Practicing Before Agency Adjudicators
- Use the Rationale Underlying the Rule
- Differences in the Use of Procedural Rules
- The Role of Administrative Procedure Acts
- Example—License Revocation by the State Medical Board
- Civil Rule 12: Defenses and Objections
- Variations in Versions of the Model APA
- Important Points

The first time many lawyers encounter an administrative hearing, they're not aware that they've slipped into the twilight zone of the law. Imagine a place where there are no rules of evidence or procedure (except those the judge deems to recognize); where there are no statutes of limitations (except those known to be useful to the agency and hostile to everyone else); where ethical double-standards abound, if indeed they apply at all; and where jurisdictional barriers are as profound as they are well hidden. All this and more await the attorney whose client innocently asks for help in dealing with an agency-run hearing. And as you'll come to know, these aren't bad things, unless they catch you by surprise.

Agencies are entrusted with adjudication authority because they're considered better suited than judicial branch courts to resolve certain kinds of disputes. What makes them better suited? Sometimes it's their expertise: while traditional judicial-branch courts tend to be generalists, executive branch adjudicators tend to be specialists. Sometimes it's the result of a legislative decision to give the lion's share of fact-finding to the executive branch, leaving only limited questions of fact and law for judicial branch determination. This might be because lawmakers trust the executive branch to carry out new laws as intended, or, more cynically, it might be because they don't trust the independent judiciary to do so. And sometimes agencies are entrusted to serve as judges because judicial branch courts have finite resources and executive agencies are better suited to handle the flood of claims likely to arise with the establishment of a new entitlement or licensing program.

The disputes that are brought to executive-branch adjudicators generally can be classified into three broad categories: disputes about governmental benefits or entitlements, disputes about licensing occupations and granting contracts for goods or services, and disputes about setting rates applicable to monopolies and utilities. The thread connecting all is found in the Fifth Amendment: when the government proposes to affect adversely a liberty or property interest, the affected parties are entitled to "some kind of hearing."[1] If our legislators entrust our executive officers to act in a way that's hostile to a liberty or property interest, the Due Process Clause guarantees a "meaningful opportunity" to be heard.[2]

Practical Differences in Agency-Run Hearings

An agency-run hearing is a creature of statute. Judicial branch courts exist because they're provided for in our federal and state constitutions. Most agencies, on the other hand, exist because our lawmakers created them. Those statutes identify the scope of the agency's power. They also let you know what kind of process the agency is required to follow when it takes action affecting a property or liberty interest. As a result, if you want to litigate before an agency, you should get to know the statutes that created it.

A core difference between trials conducted by judicial courts and administrative hearings conducted by executive-branch agencies is that agencies are not bound by the rules governing judicial courts. This is an important point, because lawyers generally receive training that prepares them to litigate in civil or criminal trial courts, which are controlled by judge-made rules of evidence and procedure. While agencies may elect to follow rules of procedure or evidence used by judicial courts, most do not. As a result, it becomes your responsibility to ferret out how the agency is going to proceed.

---

1. Henry J. Friendly, *Some Kind of Hearing*, 123 U. Pa. L. Rev. 1267 (1975).
2. Goldberg v. Kelly, 397 U.S. 254, 267–68 (1970).

Many times the agency makes this easy by including clear instructions about its process. These instructions can sometimes be found in the materials sent to your client, giving notice about the agency's proposed action. Very often instructions are also available online, through the agency's Web page.[3] The key here is to understand that you're not going to have the kind of standardization of process we find in judicial courts that use state or federal rules of evidence or procedure.

Jurisdictional Differences Based on Time

One of the more striking differences you'll encounter involves invoking the agency's jurisdiction. If your client is facing action to revoke or suspend a license, for example, you'll discover one of the most profound double standards in administrative law. In most cases, agencies have no statute of limitations requiring that they prosecute alleged license violations within a given time period. The agency can spend years developing its case, reaching back through multiple political administrations. Unless there's a specific time standard set forth in its regulations or in the enabling legislation (or in any applicable administrative procedure act), there is no bar to prosecution based on the passage of time. Equitable defenses based on time generally do not apply—so you can't count on laches.

Your client, on the other hand, probably won't be so lucky. Because agency hearings are creatures of statute, jurisdiction over a controversy is defined by those statutes. The only way a party can obtain relief through an agency's process is to properly invoke the agency's jurisdiction. If your client has ten days to file a request for an administrative hearing and you file on the eleventh, chances are the agency will decline to consider the request—and courts typically will agree. If the adjudication authority isn't timely invoked, the agency lacks jurisdiction over the subject matter, leaving your client without a remedy.

Differences in Access to Relevant Information

Closely related to this is the disparity in how cases can be prepared prior to the agency taking formal action. As discussed in chapter four, agencies typically have the authority to issue investigative subpoenas before charges are filed. It's a good practice to assume agencies have taken full advantage of this power. There would be little benefit for a regulator to tackle license violators if the evidence didn't support the charges. The supply of alleged license violators tends to far exceed agency budgets. As a result, agencies tend to prosecute only those cases most likely to produce successful outcomes for the agency. A prudent agency administrator will therefore hold on to cases until abundant evidence has been gathered. The investigative subpoena is a powerful tool in aid of the agency-driven litigation.

3. *See, e.g.,* http://www.ssa.gov/disability/ (SSA information about filing a claim seeking disability benefits, accessed 2/25/11); Hearing Under Oregon's Implied Consent Law, at http://www.oregon.gov/ODOT/DMV/driverid/ICHearing.shtml (accessed 2/25/11).

Your ability to discover relevant information, on the other hand, pales in comparison. In many instances, particularly in licensing and in health and safety cases, the investigative process itself is shielded against demands for prehearing disclosure. Moreover, many agencies permit only a narrow use of subpoenas by those outside the agency. In many proceedings, the only time you can actually require the appearance of your subpoenaed person or thing is the day of the hearing itself. As a result, your first chance at reading the document or questioning the witness may be the day of the hearing.

The disparity in resources available to gather information before the hearing is, in a way, a feature that is unique to agency proceedings. Many agency hearings are not adversarial in nature. A claimant who has been denied state welfare benefits is unlikely to obtain the services of an attorney when challenging the agency's decision. In these cases, many states create a hearing process where the agency adjudicator takes on many of the roles of the prosecutor or state's representative. The adjudicator may be called a hearing officer, a hearing examiner, an administrative law judge, or some variant of these. Here we'll refer to them as ALJs. The ALJ may be in charge of gathering evidence, of marking exhibits, of issuing subpoenas, and retaining experts. Because there frequently won't be a lawyer representing the government in these hearings, the ALJ may ask all of the questions needed to establish a prima facie case. As a result, administrative hearings take on an odd appearance, with the ALJ acting very much like a prosecutor, dressed up like a judge.

How the Scope of the Hearing Makes a Difference

Another fundamental difference between agency hearings and court trials is the scope of the hearing. Think of scope as the mandate given to an agency or a court, defining its power. That mandate is expressed differently between courts and agencies. We trust courts. We trust them to be independent of the executive and legislative powers that run our governments. We trust them to be fair, to produce a just result, to "do equity." This trust is a vital feature of constitutional grants of authority. It is expressed in part by our grant of implied powers to courts, including the granting of equitable powers. Think of equitable powers as the "recourse to principles of justice to correct or supplement the law as applied to particular circumstances."[4] That is, judicial branch courts have the power to correct or supplement statutes, regulations, and other sources of law. If black-letter law would produce an unjust result, judicial branch courts have the inherent power to correct or supplement the law, to do justice.

Agencies, on the other hand, generally lack equitable powers. This probably is no accident. When they act like courts, agencies wield incredible power. Legislators presumably understand this and build limits into the scope of an agency's authority.

---

4. BLACK'S LAW DICTIONARY 379 (8th ed. 2004).

They do this to make sure the executive branch exercises only that measure of judicial power needed to get the job done. No matter how compelling the argument, an agency adjudicator must reject the argument if it calls for the exercise of powers beyond those entrusted to the agency.

This limitation, of course, cuts both ways. Agency action that is not clearly authorized by statute can be rendered null and void. If an agency were to agree, for example, that it has jurisdiction over a case, that agreement can be rejected by courts in review if it is based on an agreement that disregards limits on the agency's power. Thus, we need to compare—line by line—the action proposed by the agency, checking to see that each such action is permitted by statute.

Similarly, it's important to distinguish between powers found in statutes and powers found in regulations. Recall that statutes are the creation of legislatures, whereas regulations are created by agencies. It is not enough for action by the agency to be permitted by a regulation; you must also determine if the regulation was permitted by statute. For example, a regulation adopted by an agency may permit the agency to issue subpoenas to compel witnesses to appear in hearings conducted by the agency. If questions arise about compliance with a subpoena, you would need to examine not only the regulation that provides for the issuance of subpoenas, but also the statute by which the legislature gave this power to the agency. If the agency's regulation exceeds the limits set by the legislature, or if there is no statute giving the agency power to issue subpoenas, you would be obliged to challenge the subpoena, even though it was issued pursuant to the regulation, because the regulation was adopted without legislative authority.

Example—The Implied Consent Hearing

In order to understand the differences between agency hearings and court trials, it helps to consider the roles of the key parties. For example, consider what happens in most states when a driver is charged with DUI. Let's say Trooper Smith arrested Jenny Jones after he concluded that she failed a roadside field sobriety test. He brought her to the station and told her to blow into a breath-testing device to determine her blood-alcohol level. She tried, but she wasn't able to provide a sufficient sample, due, she said, to her asthma. While a judicial-branch court will handle the DUI, the state department of transportation or its driver-licensing agency will likely take action against her under the state's implied consent laws. In many states, even if she's acquitted of the DUI, her "refusal" to blow into the machine will trigger an administrative license suspension against her driver's license.

Here's where the administrative proceeding gets interesting. In many states, Trooper Smith has been given authority to be the investigator, prosecutor, and jury in the suspension of Jenny's license. He conducted the roadside sobriety tests, and from this determined there was probable cause to arrest Jenny. At the station, he observed Jenny's efforts at blowing into the machine. From this, he determined on the spot that Jenny refused to comply with the implied consent law. As the investigator, Trooper Smith observed what he concluded was a half-hearted effort to blow into the machine. He then signed a preprinted affidavit, stating chapter and verse of the implied consent law, declaring Jenny's noncompliance. He then acted as both prosecutor and jury by taking away Jenny's license. To be sure, Jenny still will have her day in court on the DUI, but in most states, if she wants to get her license back she'll need to challenge Trooper Smith's action. To do this, she'll need to appear before the state driver-licensing or transportation agency.

Why Is an Agency Hearing This Case?

If you're going to handle agency adjudications, it helps to understand why the process is being held before the agency rather than in a judicial court. In our example, license suspensions historically had been included in the decisions entrusted to our judicial courts. Why change this, and why split the action between the court and the agency? Maybe it's because driver licensing is trivial when considering the more weighty matters that come before our trial courts. Or maybe it's because lawmakers cringe at the thought of judges being "soft" on drunk drivers. By shifting to the state agency the fact-finding authority needed to conduct hearings in implied consent charges, lawmakers found they could free courts of this part of controlling driver licensing, while at the same time give additional police power to the executive branch, through the state transportation department.

How Do Agencies Control These Hearings?

Control in this context comes in the form of limits on the scope of the state agency's authority when conducting the hearing. It also comes in very stringent time limitations imposed on people who want to challenge the state's action. To challenge Trooper Jones's decision to take away her license, Jenny will need to respond, usually in writing, usually within ten to thirty days. Information about these deadlines can most often be found in the correspondence sent by the agency, notifying the respondent of her right to a hearing. If not, a phone call to the agency is in order, to confirm the deadline for requesting a hearing. If she misses this deadline by even a day, chances are she'll be denied her right to appeal. Further, if she fails to exhaust administrative remedies granted to her, most judicial courts will refuse to consider challenges to the process if those challenges could have been brought before the agency.

Also, by statute, the scope of an implied consent hearing typically is very limited—much more than is the case with the DUI criminal or traffic trial. Typically, the agency's adjudicator will be permitted to consider only whether the officer had reasonable grounds for placing the person under arrest for the DUI and whether the officer explained implied consent rights and the consequence of submitting or refusing to submit to such test when the driver refused the test. If the driver took the test, the hearing will likely be limited to determining whether the test was properly administered and resulted in a prohibited BAC level.[5]

These hearings tend to be short and very narrowly drawn. In many jurisdictions, the arresting officer does not appear in person. He will submit the form that was filled out at the time of the arrest, coupled with an affidavit so that it's considered sworn testimony. If the driver wants to confront the officer, it's up to the driver to make a timely request for a subpoena. In our example, Jenny would have to know ahead of time that she wouldn't have the opportunity to confront Trooper Smith unless she requested the issuance of a subpoena.

Consider Who Will Serve as the Adjudicator

It's also important to keep in mind who the judge will be in the agency hearing. The agency's adjudicator—the ALJ—may be employed by the state transportation department or its driver-licensing bureau and might not be a lawyer. The ALJ might be working in the same office as Trooper Jones and may in fact be a former trooper or otherwise closely connected with the department. The ALJ might also be performing many of the roles we tend to expect a prosecutor or state's attorney to perform. In addition, in many administrative hearings, the ALJ will already have seen all the evidence needed to prosecute the case, even without a prosecutor present.

Find Out Who Will Represent the Government

The ALJ won't always be taking the role of the prosecutor. In some jurisdictions, the arresting officer appears, wearing two hats: he gives testimony as a witness against the driver, and then acts as the prosecutor, cross-examining the driver and any other witness. In other jurisdictions, the ALJ takes on the role of inquisitor, filling the void created by the absence of a prosecutor. This will be discussed in more detail later, but consider the impact of this feature of administrative hearings: your client will be trying to make her case before a "judge" who isn't part of the judiciary, who probably works for the agency that's prosecuting her, who may not even be a lawyer and isn't subject to any judicial or attorney code of ethics, and whose job may depend on the good will of the same people who hire and supervise the arresting officers. For many of us, this relationship among the adjudicator, the investigator, and the prosecutor is just too close for comfort.

Once the hearing begins, the ALJ will present the evidence gathered thus far. This may be the first opportunity Jenny will have to see the evidence being used

---

5. *See e.g.*, Georgia's implied consent law, O.C.G.A. § 40-5-67.1 (2002).

against her. She or her attorney will be permitted to offer evidence and question any witnesses. Recall, however, that the scope of the hearing is limited by statute or regulation. If she were to try to prove, for example, that she was not guilty of the DUI, the ALJ probably would not permit that line of questioning, unless the statute or regulation expressly allowed these questions. That's why it's so important to examine the statutes and regulations that authorized the agency to conduct the hearing. Typically, that's where you'll find a description of the scope of the hearing. I've made it a practice when litigating before any agency to contact the office and request a copy of their regulations. Without exception, agencies have been very willing to supply me with up-to-date versions of their regulations. Also without fail, these regulations provide specific references to the statutes under which the agency is operating. In addition, most agencies maintain PDF versions of their regulations online. A good example is the site maintained by the Colorado Department of Personnel and Administration's Office of Administrative Courts. Its Web site offers a complete menu of the agencies served by the state's central administrative hearing panel and has links to the statutes, regulations, and procedures used for the hearings it conducts.[6]

Differences in the Burdens of Proof

You'll also need to learn what burden of proof has to be met, who bears the burden, and whether more than one burden must be met. The burden of proof generally is established by statute or regulation. When you consult the controlling law, determine who is the proponent of an issue or claim. A party seeking to obtain workers' compensation benefits, for example, must establish a work-related injury. The controlling regulation will set out the proof needed to prevail on the claim and will identify the party responsible for establishing the presence of supporting facts. Similarly, a party claiming an affirmative defense to a disciplinary action, for example, will bear the burden of proving each of the elements of that defense. Administrative hearings tend to be regarded as civil matters, so the state has to prove its case only by a preponderance of the evidence—not with proof beyond a reasonable doubt, the criminal standard. In some instances, the government can meet its burden without producing any witnesses at all. The officer's sworn written statement—his or her version of the facts—is enough to constitute a prima facie case for the state. In Jenny's DUI case, for example, if the ALJ is an employee of the state's department of transportation, Jenny (and you) will have to convince the ALJ that there's something wrong with Trooper Smith's recitation of the sequence leading up to her blowing into the machine.

In a typical docket, Jenny's case might be one of dozens of similar cases handled by the ALJ that day. Human nature being what it is, it's easy to see how the ALJ may

---

6. http://www.colorado.gov/cs/Satellite/DPA-OAC/OAC/1194261892662 (last visited 2/25/11).

be biased in favor of certain types of witnesses. The same thing is probably true with judicial branch courts that hear high-volume cases (traffic cases, for example). But in cases tried before a judicial-branch court, you'll have the benefit of an adversarial process, and you wouldn't expect the judge to step in and present the evidence leading to your client's conviction. The administrative process permits this. It's a process that is designed to be expedient—quick and very limited in scope. Knowing what the viable issues are, and knowing who bears what burden, are essential.

The Role of Credibility Determinations

Note that the ALJ may be accustomed to giving great weight to the recitation of facts in an officer's affidavit. In such a case, the ALJ could conceivably foreclose on your client's claim based solely on what appears in the officer's affidavit. If this happens, you'll prevail only if you can establish an affirmative defense. Again, these defenses are typically found in the agency's enabling statutes or regulations. And again, proof need only be by a preponderance. The key is knowing that you must approach the ALJ fully aware of the statutes and regulations that control the hearing. You also need to acknowledge the proof that's present in the evidence already before the ALJ, challenge any invalid evidence, and add to the record enough evidence to persuade the ALJ that your client meets each element of the appropriate affirmative defense.

Realities of Practicing Before Agency Adjudicators

As you come to appreciate the unique characteristics of agency-run hearings, you'll see some things that are particularly useful. A preponderance burden, for example, can be very useful when you're trying to establish entitlement to benefits. When presenting your case, let the ALJ know which burdens your client bears, and come to the hearing with examples of cases that describe how that burden is met. Just because an agency isn't a judicial branch court, don't think the ALJ will ignore judicial precedent.

The same holds true with rules of procedure and evidence. It's true that generally agencies are loathe to adopt court rules, preferring to avoid imposing such restraints on themselves. At the same time, these rules provide rational guidance for how the ALJ should proceed. Irrational behavior gets agencies into trouble during appellate review. As such, there's a benefit in considering the policies that went into our state and federal rules of evidence and procedure. Use those policies to persuade the ALJ to reach results that are consistent with results that would occur under the civil rules.

Use the Rationale Underlying the Rule

Litigators are familiar with the rules of evidence and procedure. As we gain experience as litigators, we become familiar with both the rules and the reasons for the rules. Use this familiarity to your advantage when working with ALJs. For example, most agencies will permit the ALJ to consider hearsay. On its face, there's nothing unfair about this: the rule applies to both sides, and we've all seen times when it seems there are more exceptions to the rule against hearsay than there are stars in the sky. We know that the goal of the rules concerning hearsay is to guard against the introduction of unreliable testimony. We hope that by requiring the declarant to be present in court, we can take a more reasoned measure of his out-of-court statement.

If you're facing a hearsay issue before an ALJ, the best course of action isn't to object on the grounds of hearsay. Most ALJs will ignore the objection and many will think less of you for having made it. Instead, object on the basis that in context, the out-of-court declaration is on its face unreliable, and be prepared to explain why by noting prior inconsistencies, bias, lack of personal knowledge—whatever the circumstances warrant. In this way, you get the benefit of the hearsay rule without directly invoking it, and at the same time, you provide the ALJ with a rational basis for ruling in your favor.

Differences in the Use of Procedural Rules

Similarly, consider how useful the rules of civil procedure can be. Even though these rules generally do not apply in administrative proceedings, they can serve as excellent guides for ALJs. If you're an experienced litigator, you may well be in a position to offer procedural suggestions, particularly if the agency ALJ is either not a lawyer or not experienced in trial work.

For example, if the agency doesn't follow the state or federal rules of civil procedure, it wouldn't help to ask for discovery under Rule 26; but it might be very useful for the parties to exchange of exhibits in advance of the hearing. Knowing that you can't formally demand discovery, you can nevertheless enlist the ALJ's support in implementing a process that accomplishes many of the same things found in discovery. I've provided a sample motion that incorporates these ideas (see Appendix 1, Request for Prehearing Orders).

In one agency I've worked with, the ALJ lacked subpoena power. This wasn't an oversight; the process was very streamlined and the agency preferred to avoid judicializing their hearings. Although there was no subpoena authority, if a party wanted to compel the presence of a witness at one of our hearings, there was nothing to prevent them from writing to the person (or to the person's attorney, where appropriate), explaining why the person was needed at the hearing, and asking that they attend. I considered these efforts when determining whether to allow into evidence out-of-court statements by the witness. If the proponent of the hearsay statement showed me that they tried to get the witness to testify and the witness refused, I could take that refusal into account when determining what weight (if any) to attribute to the hearsay statement.

The Role of Administrative Procedure Acts

As you become acclimated to agency procedure, you'll discover whether your jurisdiction has an administrative procedure act (APA). APAs serve as abbreviated rules of civil procedure and evidence, and vary from state to state. The federal administrative procedure act is found at 5 U.S.C. § 551 et seq. A "Model State Administrative Procedure Act" surfaced initially in 1946 and remains in place in some states. The Model was revised in 1961 and that version was adopted by thirty states;[7] a version published in 1981 was adopted by three states.[8] These offer a template for proceeding in administrative agencies. While far less detailed than the federal or state rules of civil procedure and rules of evidence, the administrative procedure acts provide some degree of uniformity of process when appearing before administrative bodies within that jurisdiction. Thus, in preparing to appear before an administrative agency, you'll need to consult state or federal statutes to determine whether an APA applies, and if so, which version of the act is in force. After making this determination, you'll need to examine the statutes and regulations of the agency itself to determine if there are any variations from the APA applicable to the agency in question.

Example—License Revocation by the State Medical Board

Suppose your client, Martin Guzman, received a notice from the state medical board advising that it proposes to revoke his medical license. According to the notice, the Board's credentialing officer concluded your client misrepresented his educational credentials when describing his attendance at a Mexican medical school. Although the Board issued the license, it now proposes to revoke the same. After a three-year investigation, the Board has charged Martin with falsifying his academic credentials.

The first Martin learned about this decision was through a one-page notice, announcing the Board's proposal to revoke Martin's license and extending to him the opportunity to be heard. Once you invoke his right to a hearing, you trigger the Board's hearing mechanism.

At this point, you'll need to check both the Board's statutes and rules for any form of procedural provision and to determine the scope of the Board's authority.

---

7. Alabama, Arizona (in part), Arkansas, Connecticut, District of Columbia, Georgia, Hawaii, Idaho, Illinois, Iowa, Louisiana, Maine, Maryland, Michigan, Mississippi, Missouri, Montana, Nebraska, Nevada, New York, Oklahoma, Oregon, Rhode Island, South Dakota, Tennessee, Vermont, West Virginia, Wisconsin, and Wyoming. *See* CHARLES H. KOCH, JR., ADMINISTRATIVE LAW AND PRACTICE, appendix XIII at 587 (West 2d ed. 1997).
8. Arizona (in part), New Hampshire, and Washington. *See id.* at 597.

You will also need to locate the state's administrative procedure act. These should be read in tandem, although the Board's specific statutes and rules generally prevail over the more general provisions of the APA. Also, even though the Board will probably disclaim reliance on the state rules of civil procedure and evidence, open up your copy of the rules. Scanning the index, consider how some of the rules provide for procedural and evidentiary features that might be useful here.

Civil Rule 12: Defenses and Objections

As with any litigation, determine early on whether there are mandatory responses you need to keep in mind. Should you raise an objection based on adequate notice and service of the charges against Dr. Guzman? Even though the rules of civil procedure don't apply, the procedures we use in civil litigation may also arise in administrative hearings. If an issue deserves presentation before the merits hearing, fashion a response based on the premises that support protections found in Rule 12.

For example, Rule 12 provides relief when an allegation in the initial pleading is too vague or ambiguous to permit an informed response (see FRCP 12(e)). Relief here can be in the form of compelling the government to provide you with a more definite statement of the statutes and regulations at issue. It can also force the government to provide specific information about the identity of witnesses, details of the nature of factual allegations, and the disclosure or identification of documents supporting the allegations. You would not, of course, cite Rule 12 as the basis for your motion. Instead, you would consider the function of Rule 12 and argue by analogy that fair and efficient agency adjudication requires the same kind of relief. This is true, even though none of the APAs expressly permit motions for a more definite statement.

Similarly, litigation involving trade secrets, allegations of sexual abuse, and claims based on privileged or nonpublic material all may be presented in a way that instantly prejudices your client. If the Board's charging documents include sensitive material that will be subject to public disclosure, determine whether a motion to strike is warranted. Using the same rationale as is found in Rule 12(f), such a motion early in the proceeding will alert the ALJ to the need to consider shielding from public view redundant, immaterial, impertinent, or scandalous matter. Also from Rule 12, consider seeking a prehearing conference with the ALJ (see FRCP 12(i)). In all but the most routine, high-volume cases, I found prehearing conferences to be extremely valuable as a way to level the playing field during the time between when the party requested a hearing and the hearing itself.

Prehearing conferences can be important for another reason. Knowing that you will not routinely be entitled to discovery, you can use a prehearing conference to urge the ALJ to bring the parties together to narrow the focus of the hearing. If you believe your client will be at a significant disadvantage going forward without discovery, ask for a prehearing conference to make your case for prehearing exchanges of documents and witness lists. Even without the benefit of court rules, effective agency litigators can draw from those rules to help ensure a fair hearing.

Variations in Versions of the Model APA

It's important to determine whether your agency is subject to an APA, and if so, what version applies. For example, if your client seeks to intervene or prevent the intervention of a party in an agency proceeding, you'll need to determine whether an APA applies. If yours is a federal agency case, you won't find a rule directly addressing intervention in the current federal Administrative Procedure Act. Instead, the federal APA provides: "[s]o far as the orderly conduct of public business permits, an interested person may appear before an agency or its responsible employees for the presentation, adjustment, or determination of an issue, request, or controversy in a proceeding, whether interlocutory summary, or otherwise, or in connection with an agency function."[9]

The 1961 version of the Model State APA was similarly oblique, providing that "[o]pportunity shall be afforded to all parties to respond and present evidence and argument on all issues involved," and defining "parties" as "each person or agency named or admitted and entitled as of right to be admitted as a party."[10] On the other hand, the 1981 Model State APA expressly provides for intervention upon written motion showing that the petitioner's "legal rights, duties, privileges, immunities, or other legal interests may be substantially affected by the proceeding or that the petitioner qualifies as an intervenor under any provision of law" and a finding by the ALJ that "the interests of justice and the orderly and prompt conduct of the proceedings will not be impaired by allowing the intervention."[11]

In this last version, notice the provision referring to qualifying as an intervenor "under any provision of law." Typically, the agency is the source of such other "provision of law." For example, the Federal Communications Commission provides for intervention, though without using that term: "[a]ny party in interest may file with the Commission a petition to deny any application."[12] This illustrates a central lesson in understanding how to prepare for administrative litigation. Your assessment of the case has to include a determination of whether the state or federal APA applies, and if it is the former, whether the version is from 1946, 1961, or 1981. Once you determine this, if the procedural device you wish to use is not expressly

---

9. Fed. APA section 555(b).
10. Model State Administrative Procedure Act (1961), §§ 1(5) and 9(c).
11. Model State Administrative Procedure Act (1981), §§ 4-209(a)(2) and (3).
12. 47 U.S.C. § 309(d)(1); see the discussion at Jacob A. Stein, Glenn A. Mitchell, Basil J. Mezines, Administrative Law, 41-42 (LexisNexis 2007).

provided for by any APA, consider using the federal or state rules of civil procedure as a template for your requested relief.

Important Points
• Locate and read the agency's enabling statute.
• Make sure you're using the current version of the agency's regulations.
• If your issues involve prior versions of the agency's regulations, get the prior versions and include them in your motions.
• Make a chart of all applicable deadlines and identify what needs to be filed, and with whom, for each deadline.
• Find out whether the agency is subject to an Administrative Procedure Act. If it is, find out what version applies and get a copy of the whole act.
• Carefully read the notice that identifies what the agency claims your client did or failed to do. Find the full text of the appropriate version of whatever statute or regulation is invoked.
• Determine who bears which burden of proof for the core issues and for each supporting issue.
• Determine if the rules of evidence and civil procedure apply to your case.

CHAPTER TWO

EVALUATING COMPETING ADJUDICATION STRUCTURES: KNOW YOUR JUDGE AND UNDERSTAND THE ADJUDICATION STRUCTURE

> Topics in this chapter include:
>
> - The Absence of Judicial Independence
> - Judicialized vs. Institutional Agency Hearings
> - How Different Structures Impact Your Hearing
> - ALJ Independence and Fairness
> - The "Central Panel" Concept
> - Hearings Conducted By the Agency Itself
> - Important Points

One of the first things law students learn in law school is that process matters. A client can have an unquestionably valid claim, but will lose that claim if it's not timely pursued in the correct forum. As a result, law schools dedicate significant classroom time focusing on procedure. The need for this training becomes apparent the first time a novice lawyer steps into a courtroom. If she hasn't become familiar with the applicable rules, everyone in the courtroom—from the bailiff to the jury to the judge—will all know it.

The same thing can be said about first times before an ALJ. It's not hard to spot the novice representatives in an administrative hearing. They're the ones asking for discovery (which they're not likely to get), citing the rules of evidence (which are not likely to apply), and wondering when the jury will be empanelled (which is not ever going to happen). The tricky thing about administrative hearings, however, is that they tend not to have one single source of procedural rules. To acquire the skills needed to litigate effectively in administrative hearings, you need to know where to look to find these rules. To do this efficiently, it helps to find out a few things about the structure of the agency. In particular, you need to know how closely controlled the ALJ is by the agency being served.

The Absence of Judicial Independence

If you were to go to what looks like a courtroom and enter your appearance before someone who looks like a judge (i.e., she is wearing a black robe, sitting behind an impressive raised bench), you might conclude the person is a judge. If your purpose in making such an appearance is to ask for protection from government punishment or to ask for governmental benefits, you might expect that the judge is going to decide your case impartially, based on the evidence presented, without favoring the government's side of the case. That's certainly what we expect when we appear before a trial court. Our government is founded on the notion that the judiciary is independent of the executive and legislative branches. No matter how close the ties are between these three branches, judicial independence from executive- and legislative-branch controls is essential.

Once the determination of a claim or cause is entrusted to the executive branch, however, that guarantee of judicial independence vanishes. The ALJ may be unbiased, and may be limited to deciding a case solely based on the evidence presented, but by definition, the ALJ is not independent of the executive branch. By design, the process of administrative adjudication is controlled by the executive branch. It may be held in check by judicial review, and legislators may define the scope of the ALJ's authority. But it would be a mistake to believe that the black robe, the raised dais, and the courtroom environment have created an independent adjudicator.

Judicialized vs. Institutional Agency Hearings

As a litigator, your approach to agency litigation should be shaped, in part, by your understanding of the structure in which you're operating. Structures in this context vary depending on the degree of control exercised by the agency over the ALJ and over the adjudication process. At one end of the spectrum, you'll find hearings that are run by ALJs who truly are independent of the agencies they serve. While these ALJs are not independent of the executive branch of government, they are completely free of control by the agencies they serve. Professor Asimow[1] refers to this approach as a judicialized approach, because it tends to permit the ALJ to employ many of the attributes found in judicial trials.

These ALJs tend to be legally trained; they tend to be full-time employees who are not permitted to maintain private practices; they tend to be prohibited from having other duties that might compromise their ability to impartially analyze fact and law; and they tend to be bound to follow a code of ethics designed to inspire public trust and confidence in their performance. Although still part of the executive branch, and not possessing some of the important powers found in the judiciary, ALJs in judicialized administrative proceedings have significant freedom from agency overreaching and have the power to create procedural rules that guarantee a hearing that both is fair and appears to be fair.

---

1. Michael Asimow, Professor of Law Emeritus, UCLA.

At the other end of the spectrum are structures that are closely controlled by the agency, which Professor Asimow refers to as institutional proceedings. The ALJ in an institutional structure tends to be hired, paid, supervised, and disciplined by the agency that proposes to take the action being challenged. In many instances, the ALJ may wear multiple hats for the agency—serving as its rule-writer, for example, or giving advice to its investigators. Many times the ALJ in institutional proceedings isn't a lawyer. Instead, the ALJ might be someone whose background working in the agency makes her particularly useful in the fact-finding process. For example, many times people who serve as ALJs deciding welfare appeals will be experienced claims examiners. Their familiarity with welfare eligibility rules, earned during years as claims examiners, helps them make well-informed decisions when hearing appeals as an ALJ.

Of these two approaches, neither is inherently suspect, nor inherently fairer than the other. At both ends of the spectrum, the ALJ is expected to be very familiar with the agency's policies, and both are expected to be unbiased fact finders. The key differences between the two tend to involve procedural features of the decision-making process. These include differences in prehearing access to information available to the agency, differences in how thoroughly you'll be permitted to develop your case before and during the hearing, and differences in how the ALJ perceives her role in the process.

How Different Structures Impact Your Hearing

Consider, for example, Jenny Jones, who was accused of drunk driving. In all fifty states, thanks in part to federal anti-drunk-driving legislation, "implied consent" laws require drivers to submit to blood-alcohol testing if an officer has grounds to believe the driver is operating a motor vehicle while intoxicated. If a driver violates an implied consent law, there's no criminal penalty, but there is an administrative license suspension. In plain English, in obtaining your driver's license, you "impliedly" consented to taking a breath test (or having your blood or urine collected) if an officer has cause to believe you operated your vehicle under the influence. Regardless of whether you are convicted of the DUI, if you refuse to "consent" and if the officer can prove cause existed, the state licensing agency will seek to suspend or revoke your driver license.

In some states, administrative license suspensions are entrusted to the judicial branch. In Ohio and about a dozen other states, the judicial-branch courts include an implied consent feature in the DUI prosecution. In these cases, there's been no delegation of judicial power to the executive branch, and the license action remains the responsibility of the judicial courts. In all other states, the license suspension program has been delegated to the executive branch. These are called implied consent administrative license suspensions. It's important to understand which branch of government will serve as the fact finder in the implied consent part of the case.

Knowing this will help you determine what issues will be within the scope of the hearing and what deadlines apply.

ALJ Independence and Fairness

It's not, however, enough to know whether the issue will be litigated in a judicial trial or in a hearing conducted by the executive branch. If the hearing will be conducted by an ALJ, you need to know how independent the ALJ is from the agency. Knowing this will help you decide whether to have your client participate in the proceeding, and it may shape the advice you give your client regarding the likelihood of success and methods of appeal.

Human nature being what it is, most ALJs likely will tell you they're fair when they decide a case. No one who serves as a fact finder wants to think she is corrupted, biased, or incapable of providing a fully fair hearing. There are, however, structures that may tend to leave the impression that a hearing is likely to be fair, or unfair, as the case may be. Experienced litigators tend to favor ALJs who are somewhat insulated against control or overreaching by the agencies being served. The structural differences at issue here are those that concern whether the administrative hearing is to be conducted by an ALJ who is employed by a "central panel" or an ALJ who is an employee or contractor with the state agency.

The "Central Panel" Concept

In the 1980s, Maryland lawmakers sought to insulate many of its ALJs from direct supervision by the agencies being served. Rather than have the ALJs working directly for the Department of Transportation, for example, Maryland appointed a Chief Administrative Law Judge and authorized the creation of a "central panel" of ALJs. The Chief ALJ hires, trains, supervises, and disciplines the ALJs. Once the agency decides to bring charges or take action against a party, it delegates the fact-finding process to the Chief ALJ, and the Chief ALJ takes it from there.

The Maryland program, created under the guidance of the late John Hardwicke, became the model for central panels nationwide. An ALJ working under the Chief is insulated from agency control and represents the prototypical judicialized ALJ. The Maryland approach proved to be a success, trusted by litigators and by agency heads alike. It also proved to be cost-effective, because ALJs could be used wherever needed, for whatever agency being served by the panel. The ALJs are full-time employees, all with law licenses, and are subject to a code of conduct crated specifically for them. They pool their knowledge of agency policies and rotate among different state agencies according to a schedule created by the Chief ALJ.

The Maryland program became the template for the Model Act Creating State Central Panels, which has been adopted in full or in part in twenty-five states.[2] As a result, if you know your claim will be presented in a state that has adopted this Act, you'll have a significant body of procedural law to work with when preparing your case. Most central panels hear a wide variety of cases, and if a particular agency's administrative hearings are within the scope of the central panel's authority, you'll have the benefit of a centralized set of procedural rules and your ALJ will not be under the direct control of the agency prosecuting the case.

Hearings Conducted By the Agency Itself

At the other end of the spectrum are those hearings conducted by the state agency itself. Here, the ALJ is likely to be an employee of the agency that issued the citation or that can grant the benefits in issue. In these non-central panel proceedings, the procedural rules will be established by the agency, and counsel will need to determine whether the state's APA applies. These procedural rules may be antiquated and unique to the agency. They tend to be creatures of statutes that have been long neglected and are resistant to change. Where the central panel process tends to be the product of a coalescing of processes that were used by diverse agencies, processes run by agencies tend to be myopic and resistant to procedural innovations used by peer agencies.

A common complaint about agency-run hearings is that they aren't fair. This criticism comes in part from the fact that the adjudicator seems to be too closely tied to the agency to render an impartial decision. Consider the case of Dr. Guzman, who must appear before the State Medical Board. In a state where the ALJ is an employee of the Medical Board, the litigator must acknowledge some realities: she must recognize that the ALJ may have been responsible for writing the Board's rules about educational credit—rules Dr. Guzman is now forced to challenge. She must be wary of the relationship that might exist between the ALJ and the investigators who built the case against her client. She may have to explain to her client that the hearing is going to be held in the Board's office, not in a neutral location, and that key decisions about the prehearing process won't be governed by the same rules that govern civil or criminal trials.

These features of agency-run hearings are by no means universal; but neither are they unrealistic. Agencies tend to conserve their resources, selecting only sure-win cases for litigation, and settling (or not prosecuting) all others. It can be more than

---

2. *See* Christopher B. McNeil, *Executive Branch Adjudications in Public Safety Laws: Assessing the Costs and Identifying the Benefits of ALJ Utilization in Public Safety Legislation*, 38 IND. L. REV. 435, 462 (2005), citing James F. Flanagan, *An Update on Developments in Central Panels and ALJ Final Order Authority*, 38 IND. L. REV. 401, 403–04 nn. 13–15 (2005).

a little unsettling for claimants like Dr. Guzman to go forward, knowing that his "judge" is wholly controlled by the agency that is prosecuting him.

When I was working on my doctorate, the National Science Foundation awarded me a grant to study fairness in administrative hearings. Through this grant, I went to administrative hearings across the country. Half of these were conducted in central panel states; the other have were operated by the agencies. The impression I came away with was stark. Agency-run hearings tended to be dreary affairs, conducted in the bowels of bureaucratic offices by well-meaning but under-funded ALJs. In jurisdictions with central panels, I saw more openness, greater congeniality among the ALJs, and a greater sense of confidence in the system expressed by lawyers representing their clients.[3]

The purpose of the grant was to support an examination of fairness in the hearings. I conducted a national survey of participants' perceptions of fairness in their hearings. The goal was to find out if those who appear before central panel ALJs came away feeling the process was fairer than those who appeared in agency-run hearings. Generally, the evidence supported the thesis that central panels tend to produce greater perceptions of fairness when compared with agency-run hearings. Overall, however, the perception of fairness in either camp was embarrassingly low. There is a cost to ceding to the executive branch power that traditionally has been wielded by our judicial branch. In many instances, that cost comes in the form of diminished trust and confidence in the process.

Keep in mind, also, the feature of many agency proceedings by which final orders are issued. Generally, there are at least two stages of decision making in agency hearings. The ALJ, acting as a fact finder, typically will gather and evaluate the evidence and then make findings of fact. She'll then identify the relevant authority and will apply the facts to the law to reach her conclusion. At this point, the conclusion may become a final order, which can be appealed to a judicial branch court. Alternatively, the conclusion may be presented to the agency as a recommendation. In such a case, the ALJ's report and recommendation will be considered by the agency's board, commission, or department head. From there, the findings, analysis, and conclusion may be accepted or rejected by the agency, before it becomes a final order, and before judicial review may be sought. In many larger agencies, additional layers of review may exist, each of which must be activated as prerequisites to obtaining review by the judicial branch.

Understanding these steps is a critical part of successful agency litigation. You must be able to explain to your client whether the ALJ he sees during the hearing

---

3. For more detailed information and analysis see Christopher B. McNeil, PERCEPTIONS OF FAIRNESS IN STATE ADMINISTRATIVE AGENCY PROCEEDINGS: APPLYING THEORIES OF PROCEDURAL JUSTICE TO STATE AGENCY HEARINGS (Lambert Academic Publishing 2009).

is the final decision-maker, or whether interim levels of review are available prior to access to judicial-branch review. Although your ability to introduce facts sharply curtails once the first level of fact-finding ends, each of these levels of review offers opportunities to persuade your decision-maker in your favor.

Important Points

- Identify the person who will be serving as your fact finder. Learn what you can about her credentials and employment.

- Determine whether the ALJ also had a role in investigating the case or in drafting the laws she is now required to interpret.

- Be prepared to explain to your client the agency structure and the relationship between the ALJ and the agency.

- Be alert to institutional structures that may or may not make an agency's fact finder qualified to serve in your case.

- Know whether your fact finder will be rendering a final agency decision or a recommendation.

- Find out whether you are permitted to submit objections to the fact finder's report and recommendation, before it becomes a final order; and observe carefully any deadlines for filing objections.

- If the ALJ's decision is a recommendation and not a final order, find out whether you have the right to appear before the agency's final decision-maker before the recommendation is acted on.

- Be prepared at each level of review to seek to maintain the status quo by an order staying the proposed decision pending review by the judicial branch.

CHAPTER THREE

PREPARING YOUR CLIENT AND THE ALJ FOR AGENCY FACT-FINDING

Topics in this chapter include:

- Recognize the Relevant Governmental Functions
- Striking the Most Effective Litigation Stand
- The Advantages of Discovery-Free Litigation
- Anticipating Your Client's Concerns
- Collateral Uses for Agency Fact-Finding
- Limits on Constitutional Challenges at the Agency Level
- Using the Administrative Hearing as Preparation for Trial
- Preparing for Entitlement Hearings
- The Art of the Inquisition
- The Litigator's Role in an Inquisition
- Collaborating with the Inquisitor
- Practical Limitations in Entitlement Inquisitions
- The Worst of Both Worlds: Enforcement Inquisitions
- Important Points

A key element of effective advocacy is preparation. Agency litigation tends to involve governmental action, so it's important that you understand what kind of action is at stake. Executive-branch government offices can be surprisingly tricky when entrusted with judicial power. As a result, you'll be especially valuable to your client if you can explain exactly what role the ALJ will play in the fact-finding process. We'll examine agency actions involving entitlement programs later, but first, consider how to prepare your client for agency fact-finding in enforcement cases. These cases tend to look and feel a lot like criminal prosecutions. They also tend to involve adversarial behavior, with the responding parties operating from a defensive position, trying to prevent a successful prosecution of the alleged infraction.

Recognize the Relevant Governmental Functions

Because agency hearings are a blend of executive and judicial functions, take a moment to think about how best to prepare for the hearing. Consider the hypothetical case of Omar Khan, who runs a small grocery store that has a license to sell alcoholic beverages. When the state liquor-control agency receives complaints about underage sales, loitering, littering, and illegal drug sales taking place near his store, the agency concludes it has sufficient evidence to revoke this license on the ground that the store constitutes a "public nuisance."

Because it has been entrusted with adjudicating citations that are based on state liquor laws, the agency issues a written notice to Omar, identifying the facts supporting the charge and the section of law that was allegedly violated. The agency includes in this notice information about what the agency intends to do based on these alleged facts and how Omar can request an evidentiary hearing in order to challenge the proposed action.

Striking the Most Effective Litigation Stand

Given the adversarial nature of agency enforcement actions, it's prudent to take a conservative approach when preparing your client for this kind of hearing. Agencies tend to proceed only when their agents are confident that sufficient evidence has been gathered to sustain the charges against the responding party. As a result, it's prudent to be wary about being too forthcoming with agency representatives, at least until you're confident you know what they know. Acting for the respondent, you need to obtain as much of the agency's evidence as you possibly can, in advance of the hearing if possible.

Unlike criminal proceedings, where the government is obliged to disclose evidence favorable to the defendant, agency prosecutions may offer little or no prehearing disclosures. Alternatives to prehearing discovery are discussed in the next chapter, but it's important to use whatever resources you can to learn in advance of the hearing what evidence is already in the hands of the government.

The Advantages of Discovery-Free Litigation

Knowing what evidence supports the government's case, however, is only part of the prehearing process. Because formal discovery is typically not available, you're free to develop evidence that bolsters your client's position, as well as evidence that erodes the weight of evidence against your client. For example, Omar can prepare his response by securing sworn statements from witnesses who can support his side of the story. He can gather records showing his efforts at discouraging loiterers and training his staff to guard against underage sales. He can show how his use of the property is the best possible use, given the neighborhood. In short, he can develop a complete theory of the case, without sharing any of this in advance of the hearing. In the absence of discovery rules, the respondent is able to develop a proactive evidentiary base, disclosing the same only when it's clear that the ALJ will be in a position to fairly weigh the parties' competing evidentiary claims.

Apart from preparing the evidentiary base, you should also consider preparing the respondent for this kind of hearing. Not all clients can process the subtle differences between criminal and civil burdens of proof, for example. It's important, however, to explain to them that the government can prevail simply by a showing that their version of the facts is slightly more probable than the respondent's version, unlike the "reasonable doubt" test in criminal proceedings.

Anticipating Your Client's Concerns

You may also find your client is exceptionally sensitive about the collateral damage that this kind of agency action can inflict. Reputations and livelihoods often are at stake in these cases. This is particularly true when the proceeding involves an occupational or professional license, like a medical professional's license. Think of how concerned you would be if your state's disciplinary administrator charged you with violating an ethical or professional standard! Public disclosure of the charge, standing alone, can be devastating to the professional standing of your client.

Given the sensitive nature of this kind of practice, consider what your client's options are in advance of the issuance of formal charges, if you're on board before charges have been filed. After you've thoroughly familiarized yourself with the scope of the agency's authority, the nature of the charges, and the quality of the evidence likely amassed against your client, you should have a frank discussion with your client. You might find that the concern about public disclosure is foremost in your client's mind. If that's true, consider taking the initiative and contacting the agency prior to the issuance of charges.

Collateral Uses for Agency Fact-Finding

Consider also the need to prepare the case for review after the hearing. Your pre-charge assessment of the case may lead you to conclude that the agency will prevail on the merits of the case. In those instances where responding make sense, even though it's likely you'll not prevail on the merits, act with an eye towards the next stage of review. Omar may well know he's likely to lose. He and other shopkeepers with liquor licenses may have decided that now is the time to pressure lawmakers to amend the regulations controlling the sale of liquor in grocery stores. Understanding your client's goals is important, and knowing how to use the administrative hearing to advance those goals is important too. Should one goal be to mount a hallenge to the underlying regulation or statutory authority, use the agency's administrative hearing to create the factual record needed to pursue that challenge.

A good example of this arose in Ohio a few years ago. State law was enacted prohibiting smoking in public bars and restaurants. Regulatory authority was delegated to the state health department, and nominal fines were assessed against noncompliant bars. The laws were challenged in a number of ways, but one way was through the agency's enforcement process. The state health department delegated fact-finding authority to local health departments. Citations were issued to noncompliant bars, and the bars were given the opportunity to challenge the citations through a hearing conducted by the local department.

Some of these cases involved questions of fact, where the government had to prove that the owner permitted smoking—a claim that could be challenged if there was no direct evidence that the owner (through the bartender) knew someone was smoking and failed to act to stop it.[1] Generally, however, the facts were not in dispute. Instead, the responding bars challenged the enforcement of the law on procedural and constitutional grounds.[2] This feature of administrative hearings is important and frequently overlooked. As a general rule, challenges to the constitutionality of a law, or to the sufficiency of process, must be raised at the earliest opportunity. The agency's evidentiary hearing is that first opportunity. Should you fail to raise your constitutional claims at this stage, you risk losing the opportunity to do so in later stages.

Limits on Constitutional Challenges at the Agency Level

Having said that, it's important to understand the limits of mounting a constitutional challenge in an agency proceeding. Agencies generally lack the authority to find that a regulation or a statute is unconstitutional. Thus, a motion to dismiss agency enforcement action on the grounds that the antismoking law was unconstitutionally vague or the procedures violated the Due Process Clause would likely be denied by the ALJ. Like the agency itself, the ALJ generally lacks the authority to invalidate statutes or regulations. What you need to impress upon the ALJ, however, is the need to permit you to use the agency's fact-finding process as a means to create an evidentiary record that will permit reviewing courts to consider the merits of the constitutional claim.

This can be an uphill battle because evidence relevant to the constitutional claim may appear to be extraneous or only tangential to the merits claim. It will try the patience of your ALJ if you attempt to introduce evidence that you contend is necessary to prove constitutional infirmities. Anticipate this by proffering your evidence in advance of the hearing.

In the antismoking law case, for example, if you believe the process of delegating fact-finding to the local agency violates the Due Process Clause because the ALJ

---

1. Pour House, Inc., v. Ohio Department of Health, 925 N.E.2d 621 (Ohio Ct. App. 2009).
2. Deer Park Inn, Appellant-Appellant, v. Ohio Department of Health et al., No. 09AP-974, 2010 Ohio App. LEXIS 1168 (Ohio Ct. App. Mar. 10, 2010); The Boulevard, v. Ohio Department of Health et al., No. 09AP-837, 2010 Ohio App. LEXIS 1109 (Ohio Ct. App. Mar. 30, 2010); Joe Sinnett dba Joez Tabernacle Lounge v. Ohio Department of Health et al., No. 09AP-437, 2009 Ohio App. LEXIS 5837 (Ohio Ct. App. Dec. 31, 2009).

is supervised by the investigator who conducted the investigation, prepare a motion in limine and file it in advance of the hearing. State what you believe to be the salient facts, supporting this with affidavits where available. Outline the constitutional requirements, present the facts as you believe them to be, and show how the facts, if proved, establish a constitutional violation. The ALJ may accept or reject your argument, but at least you've laid the foundation to introduce the relevant evidence during the hearing. If the ALJ refuses to permit this, you have preserved your constitutional claim and your proffer can be used by the court once the agency rules against your client.

Using the Administrative Hearing as Preparation for Trial

Another important collateral value of invoking administrative process is its use as a way to discover evidence in advance of criminal litigation. As we noted in the case of our allegedly drunk driver, Jenny Jones faced both administrative and criminal charges after being arrested for drunk driving. A key value of invoking the right to an administrative hearing is that you'll have the opportunity to see some, if not all, of the evidence against your client. Equally important, if you're able to cross-examine the state's witnesses, you'll be able to get them to commit to a set of facts relating to the charge. Should the facts change at the time of the criminal trial, these changes can be brought to the jury's attention when attacking the credibility of the state's witnesses.

Understand, however, the risks that go with this strategy. Your client's presence at the administrative hearing exposes her to being called as a witness by the government. While she may wish to invoke her constitutional right against self-incrimination, there is a cost associated with doing so. Generally, the agency's fact finder is permitted to make a negative inference when a witness in an administrative proceeding invokes the protections of the Fifth Amendment against self-incrimination.[3] This means the government may question your client, under oath, seeking incriminating evidence for use in the later criminal trial. If your client refuses to answer, invoking the right against self-incrimination, the agency may infer the answers would have incriminated your client and can use this inference to find your client has violated the regulation in question.

Preparing for Entitlement Hearings

Actions like those described in the preceding hypothetical involve civil prosecutions—that is, the enforcement of disciplinary rules that are in place to protect the health and safety of the public. Not all agency hearings involve prosecutions, however. Many, perhaps most, agency hearings are designed to resolve complaints

---

3. Baxter v. Palmigiano, 425 U.S. 308 (1976); *see, e.g.,* DeBonis v. Corbisiero, 547 N.Y.S.2d 274, 276 (N.Y. App. Div. 1989).

by the responding parties, who seek a government-provided benefit or entitlement. Workers compensation hearings tend to fit in this model, as do hearings to determine whether welfare or disability benefits should be paid. Entitlement-based fact-finding by executive-branch adjudicators probably accounts for the lion's share of all government fact-finding, exceeding exponentially the combined number of cases of all kinds that are decided by trial courts of the judicial branch.

Preparing your client for entitlement hearings requires a set of skills that is significantly different from those needed in the more adversarial prosecutions of claims made by agencies against license holders. In the prosecution of disciplinary cases, you're likely to see advocates representing the government's position, just as you'd expect in a criminal case. In entitlement cases, on the other hand, it's highly likely there will be no representative from the government presenting the government's case. Instead, the ALJ has to fill that role.

The Art of the Inquisition

When there's no representative from the agency, and when the ALJ assumes the role of gatherer of information, we tend to regard the hearing as inquisitorial in nature. Inquisitions tend to have something of a bad reputation in the United States. Given how accustomed we are to the adversarial system found in trial courts, this prejudice is understandable. But inquisitions—which are very common in many modern European governmental systems—can be both effective and fair when everyone understands the role each is to play.

A frequently seen feature of inquisitorial hearings concerns the source of evidence. In a DUI trial before a judicial court, the judge starts the proceeding with a clean slate—there's no evidence on which to convict the defendant until the prosecutor presents it to the judge and asks for its admission, subject to objection by the defendant or the defendant's lawyer. In many entitlement cases, on the other hand, the ALJ arrives at the bench with all the documents that are likely to be needed for a decision adverse to the claimant. How fair is that?

In fact, it's pretty fair; at least it can be, in the right hands. Recall that in most entitlement cases, the ALJ enters the picture after the state agency announced its decision to deny a benefit sought by the claimant. Rather than hide the evidence that led to the adverse decision, the state agency is required to explain itself and to take the initiative to get this adverse evidence into the hands of the claimant. By providing the ALJ with this evidence, agency hearings ensure that the party responding to adverse governmental decision making has at least the same amount of information as was available when the initial adverse decision was made.

The Litigator's Role in an Inquisition

For the inquisitorial process to work, you need to appreciate your role as an advocate for your client. Note the term "advocate" is used here—not the term "adversary." If you approach the ALJ as an adversary, you're missing the point. Experience teaches that the best advocates in entitlement cases understand that the ALJ is vitally important as a gatherer of information.

Take the hypothetical case of Estelle Sanchez, who has been trying to receive aid for dependent children following the birth of her daughter, Ami. Estelle's earnings are sufficiently low as to qualify her for benefits. The state's department of human services, however, has refused her claim. The decision to refuse Estelle's claim was made by a caseworker at the department, who sought the identity of the child's father. Estelle knows who the father is but is afraid he will, if identified, try to take Ami to his home in Venezuela.

In the inquisition that follows, the ALJ will be provided the caseworker's file. Your job as Estelle's advocate is to examine that file, in advance of the hearing. From that examination, you will learn what standards the caseworker applied in making the decision to deny Estelle's claim. You'll also learn what facts have been developed and the source of those facts. Because this state department elected to rely on an inquisitorial process, there won't be a representative of the government arguing against Estelle. Instead, the ALJ will control the flow of information used to determine the outcome of the case.

Collaborating with the Inquisitor

You can help the ALJ gather information, just as you could in an adversarial proceeding. Working with your client, you need to identify sources of support for her position. Identify those with knowledge of the father's background, travel history, passport information, etc., and develop witnesses who can support Estelle's reasons for not wanting to disclose the identity of Ami's father. Prepare written statements for use at the hearing, obtaining signatures under oath where possible. You may elect not to use these written statements, but you should have them in the event the witness fails to appear.

You also have a role in testing the reliability of evidence that the caseworker relied on. Just because the ALJ presented the evidence, don't assume she won't also exclude evidence that had been relied on by the caseworker. The use of ALJs who are seasoned agency employees makes sense in cases like this. A seasoned agency caseworker now serving as an ALJ will be likely to spot flaws and weaknesses in the documentation being presented. If the ALJ is unsatisfied with the adequacy of the evidence, she can reverse the caseworker's unfavorable decision—even without any prompting by Estelle or you.

Practical Limitations in Entitlement Inquisitions

Sadly, another characteristic of entitlement cases is their high volume and low opportunity to provide a forum in which to be heard. Typically, you won't have much time to make your case, at least not during the docket dedicated to your client on the day of the hearing. If there is damaging written hearsay in the caseworker's file, for example, you'll have scant time to work around the damage. Accordingly, take the time in advance of the hearing to gather and present evidence that undermines the weight of the evidence that had been relied on by the caseworker. Consider filing a short (one or two page) prehearing brief, acknowledging the existence of the damaging evidence while proffering evidence that casts doubt on the damaging evidence's source or substance.

The Worst of Both Worlds: Enforcement Inquisitions

Perhaps the hardest configuration you'll confront will be where there is an inquisitorial structure for disciplinary action, and not in pursuit of an entitlement. ALJs in these cases can be under intense pressure to move cases and can be sorely restricted in the scope of evidence they can consider. Given their close association with the state agency, ALJs in non-central panel states might be especially prone to processing these cases quickly and efficiently, without taking much time to consider evidence contrary to the contents of the record prior to hearing.

Take Jenny Jones's DUI-related license suspension hearing. Cases like hers are heard by the thousands each year. Many times the arresting officer will not be personally present (unless subpoenaed by the driver). Instead of taking live police testimony, the ALJ will often have the arresting officer's affidavit and the results of any BAC testing efforts. In some states, the arresting officer does show up and is given leave to cross-examine the driver and any other witnesses. There might also be a video clip showing the events leading up to the decision to arrest for DUI.

In these cases, the degree of control exercised by the agency over the ALJ has to be taken into consideration when evaluating the risks and benefits of participating in the hearing. Ultimately, the merits of the case may be decided by the ALJ giving greater weight to one of two competing versions of events, and doing so based on factors that are impossible to discern. If an ALJ persistently gives controlling weight to an arresting officer's out-of-court sworn statement, counsel's options are few. They include prehearing motion practice designed to raise and preserve constitutional claims, challenges to the reliability of empirically based evidence (like the ability of the breath-testing machines to detect deliberate inadequate efforts by the driver), and challenges to the credibility of the state's witnesses based on internal inconsistencies and the like.

Approaching the ALJ as a collaborator in the effort to reach a just result is vital. If instead you treat the ALJ as an adversary, you'll risk shortchanging your client by losing the cooperation of the one person who controls the flow of evidence into the record of these proceedings. At the same time, experienced litigators understand the limits of what can be accomplished in this kind of hearing. To this end, the most prudent course of action, at least in implied consent cases, may well be to listen more than you speak and learn all you can about the state's case during the administrative process as a way of preparing for the criminal prosecution that will follow.

Important Points

- Take advantage of the lack of formal discovery by securing statements supporting your case and maintaining control over the evidence in your possession.

- Appreciate your client's need to remain on good terms with the licensing or entitlement agencies and avoid poisoning future relations with the agency, for yourself or your client.

- Appreciate the possibility that, through agency litigation, you may be able to impress either the agency or the legislature that changes are needed in statutes or regulations that have adversely affected your client.

- Constitutional challenges may need to be raised at the time evidence is taken at the agency level. If so, be prepared to proffer evidence supporting the challenge, even though the agency or the ALJ cannot invalidate statutes or regulations in the course of an administrative hearing.

- Consider using the administrative process as a means of both discovering the government's evidence and as a way to lock in hostile witness testimony, if your client is facing collateral civil or criminal proceedings.

- Understand the negative inferences that can be drawn when a witness invokes self-incrimination rights in an administrative hearing.

- In entitlement cases where there is no governmental representative, the ALJ will be serving as an inquisitor.

- It's OK to collaborate with the ALJ inquisitor, particularly in entitlement cases, but do so mindful of the limitations of the role played by the ALJ.

- Beware of the enforcement proceeding where the ALJ acts in the role of inquisitor. These represent real challenges in ensuring fairness in both the presentation and interpretation of evidence.

CHAPTER FOUR

PUBLIC RECORDS REQUESTS, IN CAMERA REVIEWS, SUBPOENAS DUCES TECUM, AND OTHER ALTERNATIVES TO DISCOVERY

Topics in this chapter include:

- The Importance of Transparency—Sunshine—in Governmental Action
- Transparency in Fact-Finding and Applying Facts to Law
- Three Pillars of Transparency: Public Records, Open Meetings, and Judicial Enforcement
- Accessing Evidence through Public Records Requests
- The Prophylactic Value of a Well-Phrased Public Records Request
- Agency Deliberations Before, During, and After the Hearing
- Rulemaking's Interface with Agency Adjudication
- Open Meeting Laws: Effective Use of Agency Agendas and Public Meetings
- Agency Reviews of the ALJ's Report
- Enforcement of Sunshine Laws
- The Tactical Value of Administrative Subpoenas
- Enforcement of Administrative Subpoenas
- Important Points

In one sense, agency litigation is played with cards from a stacked deck under rules that favor the house. In civil litigation between private parties, one set of procedural and evidentiary rules governs the process. Those rules were written by those with substantial experience in litigation, people who knew that to be fair, the rules had to be written so that the interests of all parties are protected. Those rules favor neither plaintiffs nor defendants and are effective as both sword and shield to litigators from all sides of the controversy.

Agency hearings, on the other hand, are conducted under rules created by one side, favoring that side. Judicial control over these rules is limited, triggered only in the case of egregious deprivations of fundamental constitutional protections. While some agencies have adopted their jurisdiction's rules of civil procedure and evidence, most have not. Instead, agency litigation is, by design, less structured, and for that reason potentially harder to prepare for.

The Importance of Transparency—Sunshine—in Governmental Action

That's not to say, however, that the respondent seeking to level the playing field in an agency proceeding is without options. Administrative litigation has as its common feature the presence of governmental action. And where there is governmental action, there is—or there should be—sunshine. Sunshine, in this context, is emblematic of the notion that in a democratic republic, the government works for the people. Long before there were governmental agencies with the power to take away property or liberty, there were rules ensuring transparency in governmental actions. Sunshine in government means access to information held by the government, and it means openness in governmental decision-making.

Openness, transparency, sunshine, these are truly wonderful features of governmental activities. Consider, in contrast, what happens to the decision-making process in a criminal or civil trial where a jury decides the case. Once the evidence is presented and the jury adjourns to deliberate, the door is closed. Absent some tightly controlled rules permitting special verdicts and polling of jurors, the civil and criminal trial process permits no light into the deliberative process of our juries. The same is true with many bench decisions, rendered immediately after the last witness finishes testifying, by a judge whose docket is long and who has no time (or obligation) to explain his findings.

Transparency in Fact-Finding and Applying Facts to Law

Administrative decision-making, on the other hand, is designed to be transparent. A key feature of the process is the manner in which the decision itself is presented. Under most administrative procedure acts, the ALJ must set forth findings of fact and conclusions of law.[1] In this very simple way, the parties, the public, and reviewing courts in the judicial branch can evaluate the substance on which the agency has rendered its final order. In a bench trial in the judicial branch, the judge is authorized to determine guilt or innocence, to grant or deny a tort claim, to make any number of final and binding orders, all without explanation or articulation of why and how the decision was rendered. Similarly, when juries decide cases in criminal or civil trials, their entire work product typically is presented in a verdict of a single word or sentence. Agency proceedings require more than that. They require written or oral predicate findings—findings of parts that constitute findings of the whole.

---

1. *E.g.*, Ohio Rev. Code § 119.09 (2010).

Three Pillars of Transparency: Public Records, Open Meetings, and Judicial Enforcement

Apart from this important form of transparency, agencies are obliged to open their doors in other ways as well. Administrative litigators need to familiarize themselves with three main vehicles for gaining access to information when protecting their clients' interests. First, they need to understand and master laws providing free access to publicly held information. Second, they need to determine whether decision making that led to the agency's action was subject to laws requiring public business to be conducted exclusively during open, public meetings. And third, they need to be prepared to compel the production of evidence that is not subject to public records or open meetings laws, where such evidence is necessary to protect their clients' due process rights.

Accessing Evidence through Public Records Requests

Unlike civil trials, where access to information controlled by the opposing party is regulated by civil discovery rules, an agency hearing may or may not have rules requiring a mutual, prehearing exchange of evidence. Even if there are rules providing for such an exchange, however, the litigator needs to be prepared to use public records laws as an essential tool to gather all relevant information in advance of the hearing. Generally, you'll find these in the jurisdiction's statutes under the heading of public records.[2] Another resource is the state attorney general's office. The Texas Attorney General, for example, publishes an open meetings handbook and a public information handbook that provide a comprehensive review of public records laws for that state.[3]

Note that these rules apply to any requestor. You don't need to be involved in litigation to compel an agency to disclose records under these laws. This means that, working with your client, you can identify likely sources of records that might be used against the client during an enforcement action, for example. By making a public records request, you can begin to assemble those documents that might later on be introduced as exhibits against your client. It also means that you can start your preparation long before the agency actually files a charge against your client.

Consider, for example, Dr. Guzman. The state medical board is proposing to revoke his medical license because of irregularities with his credentials, obtained while a student in a Mexican medical school. He has learned that the application he filed with the state medical board is now being used to show he misrepresented his educational background. As counsel, you need to be sure you know exactly what that application shows. It shouldn't surprise you to find that your client won't have

---

2. *E.g.*, Nevada Rev. Stat. 239.001, *et seq.*
3. https://www.oag.state.tx.us/oagNews/release.php?id=1342 (accessed 2/25/11).

kept a copy of this application, but even if he did, you'd still need to see what the board's records show. At the first hint that there might be a problem with this application, long before the board decides to act, you can request copies of those records relating to your client. Further, unless they are protected by some specific provision of state or federal law, records of other applicants to the same school may be accessible, along with records showing whether the board has treated in the same manner all applicants with these credentials.

This is not to suggest that you should expect to find the agency's "smoking gun" evidence using public records laws. Exculpatory evidence—evidence highly prejudicial to the state's case and useful to your case—may indeed exist, but if it does, you might be hard pressed to find it through any public records request. Such evidence is usually acquired by the agency through its investigative agents. Public records laws typically exempt from disclosure documents obtained through the investigative process. The federal Freedom of Information Act, for example, exempts from public disclosure "information compiled for law enforcement purposes," including information that could "reasonably be expected to disclose the identity of a confidential source," or would "disclose techniques and procedures for law enforcement investigations."[4] A complete list of exemptions is included as Appendix A.

The Prophylactic Value of a Well-Phrased Public Records Request

Even in those cases where you're not aware of the existence of any public records relevant to your client's case, consider making a public records request as a matter of course. Requests for records maintained by federal agencies can be made online through a Freedom of Information Act Web site.[5] When dealing with state agencies, look for open records resources within the agency or, more frequently, within the state's attorney general's office. Arizona, for example, has a public records citizens' aide, who maintains a Web site to assist public records seekers.[6] In the absence of such a resource, your request should be in writing, directed to the agency in question, and should be sufficiently focused to permit the agency to understand whose records you are seeking and the relevant timeframe for the request. Requesting all records pertaining to Dr. Guzman's application, for example, would (or at least should) trigger a review by the medical board's staff to see if there are any records identifying Dr. Guzman that are covered by the state's public records law. In its review, the board's staff will need to determine whether any such record is subject to an exception. In any event, the board should respond to your request, advising whether such records exist and if any exemptions apply. During the hearing, if you

---

4. 5 U.S.C. § 552(b)(7) (2006).

5. http://www.justice.gov/oip/other_age.htm (last visited 2/25/11).

6. http://www.azleg.gov/ombudsman/public_records.html (last visited 2/25/11).

encounter documents that were not identified through your public records request, use the response you received from your earlier request to prevent the introduction of any information wrongfully withheld.

Note, however, that most public records laws contain no clear exclusionary-rule type of provision calling for the suppression of wrongfully withheld evidence in administrative hearings. Just the same, there is value in making the effort to find such evidence. In my experience as a state agency hearing examiner, the attorney who has taken the trouble to make a public records request achieves two important goals. First, she demonstrates her understanding of the need to compensate for the lack of discovery in agency hearings. By using all appropriate tools for gathering information in advance of the agency's hearing, she's proved that she knows her way around agency litigation.

Second, her efforts lend meaningful weight to motions she may make during the hearing that concern the wrongfully withheld evidence. If, for example, she made a proper public records request for statements made by or about your client and received no response (or a response indicating that no such documentation exists), I would be inclined to sustain her objection to the government's use of such evidence during the hearing, at least in the absence of a very good explanation for why the evidence was withheld. At the very least, I would regard favorably a request for a continuance, if the withheld evidence was substantial and if she needed time to respond properly to it.

Agency Deliberations Before, During, and After the Hearing

Another sunshine law concerns the deliberative process of the agency itself. Generally, when a governmental agency acts, its action is recorded. When the head of the state department of education, for example, determines that all public school teachers need to have at least a bachelor's degree, the action must be published. The rule-making process, while beyond the scope of this book, is thus an important feature to consider when engaging in administrative litigation. If rule-making procedures were not followed when called for, enforcement action based on those rules may be rendered void by reviewing courts, if not by the agency itself.

Don't overlook the political side of governmental agencies. Large departments, like state welfare, transportation, and education agencies, tend to be operated under the direction of a cabinet-level appointee. These individuals most often attain their position through a political process whose key feature is public association with the elected official. It can be exceptionally embarrassing for a governor, for example, to learn that his appointed secretary of education has promulgated and adopted a residency requirement, only to find the rule needs to be invalidated due to errors in the rule-making process. The seasoned advocate, representing the interest of a teacher facing termination because he cannot meet the residency requirement, would know to approach the state agency's counsel, seeking to resolve the matter without a public hearing. By discretely raising a legitimate, well-founded claim that exposes a defect in the rule-making procedure, the teacher's attorney can protect the client's interests while permitting the agency to cure the defect outside the glare of a public disciplinary hearing.

Rulemaking's Interface with Agency Adjudication

Note that such an approach is dependent on the existence of a well-founded claim of rule-making error. In the example above, assume your research establishes that the state department of education is under the direction of a secretary of education. If your client sought to fight the rule's application, you would want to determine whether the department published the rule, extended the necessary opportunity for comment, considered in a meaningful way any comments submitted during the comment period, abided by all time requirements, and in all other respects met each of the requirements found in the administrative procedure act's rule-making provisions. You might be surprised to find that the "rule" relied on by the department is in fact nothing more than something that appeared in a memorandum circulated among mid-level functionaries and has never been subject to notice and comment. If that's the case, you'll need to research your jurisdiction's rule-making jurisprudence to determine whether the agency actually has the authority to enforce its mandate, given the failure to comply with rule-making provisions of the jurisdiction's administrative procedure act.

In the prior example, the government acted through a department head, the state's secretary of education. When governmental departments promulgate rules, public comment is routed through the rule-making process. The deliberative part of this process is supposed to include a conscientious consideration of comments received during the public comment period. In this way, agencies act like micro-legislatures, in that they are expected to deliberate on the wisdom of their proposed rule, taking into account the diverse views of those with an interest in the regulation, who take the trouble to file comments during this time. An agency that skips this step or disregards public comments does so at the risk of having the rule invalidated by judicial-branch courts.

Open Meeting Laws: Effective Use of Agency Agendas and Public Meetings

Not all agency deliberations, however, take place through the rule-making process. Many decisions affecting property or liberty interests take place during the formal assemblies conducted by the agencies, typically during meetings of the board or commission. Conducting public business is itself a highly regulated activity, and those regulations need to be taken into account whenever determining the legitimacy of the government's conduct.

Consider, for example, Dr. Guzman and the state medical board, which is seeking to terminate his medical license because of alleged defects in Dr. Guzman's medical school credentials. Typically, when any public board or commission meets to discuss public business, their deliberations are subject to open meetings laws. Long before Dr. Guzman filed his application for licensure in his state, members of the medical board likely were conducting public meetings. During these meetings, they may well have discussed rules for licensing candidates from foreign medical schools. Those discussions probably fall within the state's open meetings laws. Common requirements found in open meetings laws include the public posting of the agenda of upcoming board meetings, the taking of minutes, and the identification of votes on motions presented.

In this example, Dr. Guzman's lawyer would want to examine when the credentials requirements had been discussed by the board; whether the subject was included in the agenda for that meeting; whether the agenda was posted and publicized in the manner required by the open meetings law; and whether the minutes of the meeting were recorded in the state's register or other compendium showing a record of the results of open meetings. The attorney would also want to confirm whether each voting member was qualified to cast a vote and whether there is any reason to believe the voting members deliberated outside the public view, in violation of the open meetings law.

Violations of open meetings laws can arise when members of a board or commission act surreptitiously, deciding an official course of action in a way that improperly excludes the public. An example of this would be the round-robin phone meeting, where the members of a board or commission discuss board business, one at a time, until all members have agreed upon a course of action on a given agenda item. At the public meeting, there is little or no discussion, and the agreed-upon course of action is taken without any of the give and take we expect when important decisions are made. Were the rules under which Dr. Guzman was being charged promulgated and approved in this fashion, the rules could be challenged as void, although such a challenge likely would need to be made in civil court.

In this context, it helps to distinguish between two kinds of decision-making by boards. Consider whether the proposed action is designed to affect a broad population or is targeting only one stakeholder. If, for example, the state medical board wants to enhance the credentials needed for accreditation by foreign medical schools, this suggests the board seeks to affect a broad population, and thus is engaging in rule making. Its actions in such a case would have to conform to both the rule-making requirements of the state's administrative procedure act and the state's open meetings law. On the other hand, if the board's action is based on its determination that a particular course offered by the Mexican medical school was a sham, the determination is not broadly made, but is narrowly tied to one course by one school. In such a case, rule making is not required, and the board may act through its adjudication process.

Agency Reviews of the ALJ's Report

Another way open meetings issues arise is in the deliberation of members of the board in individual cases. These are similar to jury deliberations, occurring once the fact-finding process is completed. In many jurisdictions, members of licensing boards will delegate the fact-finding process to an ALJ. Once the hearing is completed, the ALJ issues a report to the board, with findings of fact, conclusions of law, and a recommendation. This process is akin to the use of special masters or magistrates in courts of appeals, when those courts are called upon to engage in fact-finding. The ALJ convenes the parties, hears their evidence, and issues a report, which then is presented to members of the board.

Once the ALJ has heard the evidence, described the controlling law, and issued her recommendation, the board deliberates on the recommendation before issuing a final order. The board members are expected to consider the merits of the report, and in most cases, that deliberation is not exempted from open meetings laws. Were the board members to discuss this privately, in violation of the applicable open meetings law, the results of their deliberation could be subject to challenge.

It should, perhaps, be understood that it is exceptionally difficult to prove violations of open meetings laws. One would not reasonably expect a board member to confess to having discussed board business with his fellow board members while having drinks at a bar the night before the board meeting. Nevertheless, effective advocacy includes keeping an eye out for significant irregularities in the deliberative proceedings of agencies. If, for example, you attend the open meeting of a board when it has your client's case before it, you should expect some open discussion about the merits of the ALJ's recommendation. A board that simply decides the question without publicly discussing the issues relevant to the case may well have taken the deliberative process underground.

Thus, there are two well-hidden features of agency litigation to keep in mind when evaluating the sustainability of action taken against your client. First, determine whether the regulations cited in the prosecution of your client were published in accordance with the APA's rule-making process. Second, determine whether the deliberative body that charged your client complied fully with the applicable open meetings laws. Noncompliance with open meetings laws is a serious matter, and the actions taken through such noncompliance may be void.

Enforcement of Sunshine Laws

Note that generally, the ALJ presiding over your client's administrative hearing will not be able to enforce your client's rights under the public records or open meetings laws. The ALJ does not have plenary power—such power is circumscribed by the authority delegated to the agency from the legislature, and enforcement of sunshine laws tends to be retained by the state's attorney, rather than individual state agencies. Also, it's not realistic to think that the agency would admit to deliberately violating these laws, and in the real world, it is unlikely that the ALJ would be in a position to ferret out proof of noncompliance, particularly where the ALJ is an employee of the agency and is subject to supervision by the very people who might be inclined to circumvent sunshine laws.

Nevertheless, if you have good cause to believe a violation of sunshine laws has occurred, it is incumbent on you, as the respondent's representative, to make a record of the evidence supporting your allegations. You need to be prepared to show when, how, and by whom these laws were violated. You also may need to raise these concerns at the earliest opportunity, or risk waiving rights based on those claims. It is also incumbent on you to investigate fully and fairly such allegations before giving voice to them. Specious, hyperbolic, and unfounded claims of violations of sunshine laws damage a lawyer's reputation quickly and oftentimes irretrievably.

The Tactical Value of Administrative Subpoenas

There is one more resource available to the administrative litigator when preparing to present evidence at a hearing. Most agencies, but by no means all, have subpoena authority. This authority takes two forms—the investigative subpoena and the subpoena to compel the appearance at a hearing. Both are creatures of statute, and in the absence of express authority, it is unlikely such power can be inferred. For example, the United States Department of Agriculture's inspectors have been authorized to issue a subpoena in connection with an investigation being conducted by the Department, and may "compel the attendance of witnesses and the production of evidence relating to the investigation may be required by subpoena at any designated place, including the witness' place of business."[7] At an administrative hearing, the ALJ presiding over cases brought by the Department has the power to "issue subpoenas as authorized by the statute under which the proceeding is conducted, requiring the attendance and testimony of witnesses and the production of books, contracts, papers, and other documentary evidence at the hearing."[8]

---

7. 7 CFR 1.29(a) (2010).
8. 7 CFR 1.143(2)(c)(4).

Investigative subpoenas permit agencies to compel the appearance of persons and the production of evidence, in advance of the hearing and in advance of charges being filed. This gives the agency extraordinary power, and often it is used with great relish. The investigative process tends to be closely guarded and intractable. Outsiders to the investigative process are generally not welcome, and once an investigator determines a violation has occurred, it can be very difficult to change minds. Investigators are generally free to choose their targets and are not required to obtain judicial-branch warrants under most conditions. As a result, the agency's power to gather evidence in advance of the hearing, indeed, in advance of charges ever being filed, far exceeds that available to counsel for the respondent.

The second type of subpoena authority arises in the context of agency litigation, once charges have been filed or agency action adverse to your client has been proposed and the opportunity for a hearing arises. This type of subpoena permits a party in the agency litigation to use the power of the agency to compel the appearance of persons and the production of evidence for use at the hearing. Again, this power is not inherent—it must be expressly granted to the agency by the legislature. Use of this power permits you to compel the appearance of witnesses, even those hostile to your client. It also permits you to compel government witnesses to appear and bring with them those records used to build the case against your client.

Enforcement of Administrative Subpoenas

It would be naive to conclude, however, that invoking the power to subpoena records or hostile witnesses will actually result in the appearance of either the witness or the document. Generally, agencies have not been given the power to enforce subpoenas. That power is typically retained by courts of the judicial branch, which also are blessed with the power to hold in contempt those who fail to comply with subpoenas. As a result, if you obtain a subpoena from the agency, and the subpoena compels the appearance of an investigator or undercover agent, for example, what happens if the target fails to appear? Not much, in many cases.

Technically, you should file a motion asking the agency to enforce the subpoena. This generally is done by someone from the agency filing a petition in civil or criminal court seeking the enforcement of the agency's subpoena. You can probably imagine how infrequently that happens. An agency that believes your client has violated its regulations is not going to be eager to direct one of its lawyers to file a lawsuit in civil court for the benefit of your client. That doesn't mean, however, that you should disregard the matter, nor does it suggest you should skip this step altogether. By demanding, where appropriate, that the agency issue subpoenas and then moving for enforcement of any subpoena not complied with, you lay the necessary foundation for future action that may prove exceptionally helpful to your client during the evidentiary hearing and in any later appeal.

For example, if the witness you seek is considered friendly and the witness fails to appear, requesting the subpoena might be the only way you'll convince the ALJ to delay the hearing so that you can try to obtain compliance through informal means. If the target was hostile, the refusal to abide by an agency order is a basis to suggest the witness's contempt for the agency. That, in turn, may compel the ALJ to give less weight to any evidence the government may have acquired from the witness. And hostile or friendly, the noncompliance may prove to be sufficiently relevant to your client's due process rights to convince a reviewing court to overturn any adverse agency action on appeal.

Important Points

- Agency adjudication is based on agency action, and agency action generally must be transparent.

- Sunshine laws establish your right to access information held by governments.

- You don't need to be engaged in litigation to get the benefit of sunshine laws.

- Sunshine laws include laws that require access to public documents and records, and that require public business to be conducted during meetings that are publicized and are open to the public.

- Agency regulations and those rules intended for general application need to be promulgated through an open rule-making process.

- Check to make sure the regulations being used as a basis for agency action against your client were promulgated in accordance with the applicable administrative rule-making procedure.

- Make a practice of requesting all public records held by the agency pertaining to your client.

- After an evidentiary hearing, the agency's deliberation of an ALJ's report generally needs to be conducted in a public proceeding.

- Be alert to agency actions that circumvent public records or public meetings laws. If you see something, say something.

- Use subpoenas for both friendly and hostile witnesses: if the former fail to appear, the subpoena will support your request for a continuance or the use of hearsay. If the latter fails to appear, the subpoena will support your objection to using any hearsay from that witness.

- In appropriate cases where a critical witness has failed to comply with a subpoena, move the ALJ to seek an order of enforcement through the judicial-branch court.

Chapter Five

Recognizing the Limits of Evidentiary Hearings before Government Agencies

> Topics in this chapter include:
>
> - Your Client's Perception of Fairness in the Administrative Process
> - Due Process Theories Applied in Administrative Adjudication
> - Creating a Due Process Checklist—The Mathews v. Eldridge Standard
> - The Constitution's Cost-Benefit Approach to Due Process
> - Identify the Source of the Property or Liberty Interest
> - Appreciating and Explaining the Risk of Harm
> - Demonstrate the Efficacy of Your Proposed Alternative Process
> - Assess the Costs Associated with the Procedural Safeguard Being Sought
> - Important Points

Most experienced litigators know this to be true: the more your client believes his cause was fairly understood and the evidence was fairly presented and considered, the more likely the client will have confidence in your work and in the legal system generally. Win or lose, we all tend to care deeply about how we're treated when we're involved in litigation. If we believe all sides to a dispute have an equal opportunity to have their points of view presented, and that we're equally benefiting from procedural rules and practices, then we're likely to perceive the result as being just and fair.

Administrative agency litigation has some features that tend to create imbalances between the government and the governed. Agencies operating in states where there is not a modern administrative procedure act, for example, can create rules that clearly favor the government. This can take the form of limits on prehearing exchange of evidence, restrictions on the ability to compel the presence of witnesses, and other rules or practices that provide less procedural protection to those challenging the government.

Your Client's Perception of Fairness in the Administrative Process

There are two reasons it is particularly important to be aware of the limits of evidentiary hearings before government agencies. The first concerns your relationship with your client, as you prepare him for his hearing. Obviously, you want to be sure you accurately describe the process to him—that you don't make unfounded claims about the steps you'll be taking to prepare for the hearing. I've seen far too many instances where unknowing lawyers appear at a prehearing conference with their client in tow, and use the conference to trigger the start of a discovery schedule, only to be told there will be no discovery prior to the hearing. Avoid this embarrassment by familiarizing yourself with the rules under which the hearing will be conducted. Being candid with your client, without being overly cynical, can go a long way in establishing reasonable expectations about what will, and what will not, be accomplished by going to hearing.

The other reason for understanding the limits of evidentiary hearings has more to do with reviewing courts than with either your client or the agency itself. Reviewing courts are the true check against abuses of agency power. If you believe the process is so skewed in the agency's favor as to deny your client's protected rights, then it will be to the courts that your energies will be focused. In order to invoke effectively the reviewing power of the judicial branch, it's important to understand the constitutional benchmarks that help determine how much "process" is "due."

Due Process Theories Applied in Administrative Adjudication

To understand the analysis courts undertake when evaluating claims that an agency's process is constitutionally infirm, consider the example of Esther Lett. Ms. Lett had four children, ages three months to fifteen years. All received public assistance, but that assistance was abruptly terminated on February 1, 1968. The state welfare administrator terminated these benefits based on a report that Ms. Lett was employed by the local board of education. In fact, Ms. Lett worked for Operation Head Start on twenty-six different days between July and August of 1967, earning $300; all of which was known to the local welfare agency. The factual error here was to be found in the employment report submitted by the board of education, which mistakenly reported Ms. Lett was employed after August 1967. For whatever reasons, the board refused repeated requests by legal aid lawyers to correct its error unless the welfare agency requested a new verification.

In the meantime, Ms. Lett was forced to live on the handouts of friends and neighbors; she and her family were hospitalized after becoming ill from eating spoiled food donated by a neighbor; and her request for emergency assistance yielded $15 to feed her family until the matter could be heard. Key to this case was the procedural feature by which the welfare agency was authorized to terminate the welfare payments prior to permitting the claimant to present her case in a hearing.

Ms. Lett's case was one of several that formed the factual background for the Supreme Court's decision in *Goldberg v. Kelly*.[1] Goldberg became the benchmark decision in agency litigation and expresses the Court's standards concerning due process in agency hearings: that in entitlement cases, the Due Process Clause requires the recipient be afforded an evidentiary hearing before the termination of benefits. The Court is interested in whether the claimant is at risk of suffering "grievous loss" and balances that risk against the "government's interest in summary adjudication."[2]

Creating a Due Process Checklist—The *Mathews v. Eldridge* Standard

It is this balancing of the risk of private injury on the one hand, against the benefits of expedient governmental decision-making on the other, which is the hallmark of judicial review of agency procedural protections. Accordingly, in representing your client's interests, a successful challenge to inadequate process will depend on your ability to describe fairly (1) the risk of loss or harm incurred by an agency's process, and (2) the insupportable nature of the government's interest in expedience.

In *Goldberg*, the agency argued that its existing process allowed for a post-termination "fair hearing" and authorized repayment of any benefits wrongfully denied during the review. The risk of harm here, however, was too great, where the agency's process would tolerate the wrongful cessation of benefits that the Court said were "the very means by which to live"[3] while the issue was being litigated.

Case law since *Goldberg* has shaped and reshaped its tenets to a degree. Entitlement cases, particularly those in which the poor and disabled seek support for essentials needed for daily living, tend to generate decisions that ensure "some kind of hearing" is provided for prior to implementation of the proposed governmental action. Six years after *Goldberg*, in *Mathews v. Eldridge*, 424 U.S. 319 (1976), the Court provided a more detailed description of the test courts are to use when evaluating due process claims associated with agency litigation. Courts are to consider three factors: "First, the private interest that will be affected by the official action; second, the risk of an erroneous deprivation of such interest through the procedures used, and the probable value, if any, of additional or substitute procedural safeguards; and finally, the Government's interest, including the function involved and the fiscal and administrative burdens that the additional or substitute procedural requirements would entail."[4]

---

1. 397 U.S. 254 (1970). *See Kelly v. Wyman*, 294 F.Supp. 893, 899–900 (S.D.N.Y. 1968).
2. 397 U.S. 254, 263.
3. 389 U.S. 235, 239.
4. 424 U.S. 319, 335.

The *Mathews* test continues to be the benchmark used by courts to determine the merits of constitutional challenges to the fairness and adequacy of agency process.[5] Note that in *Mathews*, the test yielded an outcome favoring the agency, not the claimant, where the Court found that an evidentiary hearing was not required prior to the termination of disability benefits, as long as such a hearing was provided for before the termination order became final.

The Constitution's Cost-Benefit Approach to Due Process

It's important to understand the implications of the balancing required under *Mathews*. In some respects, the test justifies giving more "process" to wealthier, better-placed individuals like doctors, and less to the unskilled, or the poor, sick, and homeless. If the "private interest that will be affected by official action" takes seven years of study and costs scores of thousands of dollars to obtain (as would be the case with a medical degree and license), that interest may command a right to discovery, whereas a truck driver facing the loss of her livelihood upon the revocation of a commercial driver's license may get nothing more than a perfunctory fifteen minute hearing on the question of whether she violated a state's implied consent laws.

This cost-benefit feature of due process analysis cannot be overlooked when evaluating the adequacy of the procedural structure under which your client's claim will be heard. Under *Mathews*, your chances of successfully challenging an agency's process improve to the extent (1) you can demonstrate that your client has a private interest and that it's being threatened by the agency's action; (2) there is a risk of the agency reaching an erroneous and prejudicial outcome given the procedures they presently are using; (2 ½) the suggestions you're offering to supplement or change the existing process really would help reduce the risk of a mistake prejudicial to your client; and (3) it's not going to cost the government, in time, resources, or money, to implement your proposed substitute procedures.

Identify the Source of the Property or Liberty Interest

With respect to the first factor, note that the Fifth Amendment, and its Due Process Clause, do not by themselves bestow a protectable interest. For the Due Process Clause to be successfully invoked, you need to identify either a property or a liberty interest that would be threatened by the proposed agency action. Ms. Lett, for example, could not point to the Fifth Amendment as the source of her entitlement; instead, she would need to show that state welfare laws exist and that under those laws she was entitled to benefits. The Due Process Clause is then invoked while citing to the welfare statute, describing Ms. Lett's interest in continuing to receive benefits, showing where in the statute Ms. Lett reasonably is entitled to benefits and noting the agency's written intention to terminate those benefits. Remem-

---

5. *See e.g.*, Hamdi v. Rumsfeld, 542 U.S. 507 (2004).

ber to begin any discussion about Due Process rights by a description of the source of rights—be it a statute, an agency policy or regulation, a contract, or some other recognized source by which property or liberty interests are bestowed.

Appreciating and Explaining the Risk of Harm

With respect to the second factor, here's where your skill as an advocate comes to the fore. Risk of harm, like beauty, may well be in the eye of the beholder. ALJs who have been embedded in an agency for time immemorial may be blind to the risk of harm associated with "business as usual" at the agency. For some ALJs, the fact that the agency has always done something in a given way is ample evidence that it's not prejudicial to your client. Your job, if the facts support it, is to show how the current process makes it impossible for you to secure a fair hearing for your client. For example, consider the licensing board that sends out a notice of proposed charges that does not identify by date when your client's alleged misconduct occurred. There may be no prior experience whereby an attorney asked for what amounts to a bill of particulars—i.e., a more definite statement of the facts supporting the charge and the authorities under which the charge was brought. Your job is to show how this information is needed for your preparation and defense of your client, so that the ALJ can see the risk that he'll erroneously find against your client under the process that is currently in use.

Demonstrate the Efficacy of Your Proposed Alternative Process

Coupled with the second factor—at stage two and a half—is the need to convince the ALJ that your proposed alternative would actually help ensure an error-free hearing. Make your case by explaining the likely benefits of your proposed change in the process: how will it help, who will it help, and will it add to or take away from the efficient development of the record needed by the ALJ.

Assess the Costs Associated with the Procedural Safeguard Being Sought

The third factor is just as important as those that precede it. You need to anticipate what the practical and logistical impact of your proposal would be on the agency. What will it cost, in time, in agency labor, in the ALJ's own docket? Your chances improve to the extent you can demonstrate that the proposed changes would streamline the evidence-gathering stage of the hearing, would enable all parties and the ALJ to focus on only the true areas of contention, and would reduce wasted time for any or all the participants.

Note also that these are steps you should take at the hearing or prehearing stage, not for the first time on appeal. As I've noted earlier, it is true that agencies cannot invalidate statutes. As such, you may be tempted to buy into the argument that there is no place in the administrative hearing itself for your claims of due process violations. The better course, however, is to raise your objections to constitutional infirmities at the earliest possible opportunity, or risk having a reviewing court deem those objections waived. This means that you come to the hearing, or prehearing conference, armed with a written motion that includes citations to *Mathews* and your jurisdiction's adoption of the *Mathews* holding, with each of the three factors clearly set forth, and with a factual proffer (through affidavit if appropriate) in support of your arguments. That way, if the ALJ is indifferent to your protestations, you have made a clear record of the constitutional claim early on, and can refer back to it if the matter has to be considered by a judicial court on appeal.

Important Points

- Identify the property or liberty interests applicable to your client's case—and be able to cite to the authority that supports these interests. Without it, there are no Due Process rights.

- Be prepared to explain to your client, accurately and in plain English, the process the agency will follow.

- The level of process that is due is dependent in part on the private interest that will be affected by governmental action. The more valued the private interest, the more process will be due.

- Be able to describe the risk of an erroneous deprivation that exists with the agency's current process. What harm is likely to come to your client if the agency proceeds in the manner intended, and where is the risk that the agency will be making a mistake in taking the approach?

- Be prepared to offer a suggestion for improving the process and to show how your suggestions will reduce the risk of mistaken action by the agency.

- Make a realistic assessment of the cost (in time, money, public safety, etc.) of your proposed improvement in the process, and be prepared to show how your approach involves minimal costs and provides a way of reducing the risk of agency error.

- At its core, the Due Process Clause requires a cost-benefit analysis. You're likely to prevail if you can show that your suggested procedure reduces the risk of the agency making a mistake while at the same time incurs minimal costs to the agency.

CHAPTER SIX

BEST EVIDENTIARY PRACTICES FOR AGENCY LITIGATION

Topics in this chapter include:

- The ALJ's Duty to Marshal the Evidence and Create a Record
- A Cautionary Tale—The Litigator's Duty to Create a Clear Record
- Transcripts and Recordings
- Preparing Evidence for Admission at the Hearing
- Consider Seeking a Prehearing Evidentiary and Procedural Order
- Using Motions in Limine
- Official or Administrative Notice
- The Residuum Rule and Over-Reliance on Administrative Notice and Hearsay
- Scientific and Technical Evidence, and the ALJ as Gatekeeper
- Important Points

By its nature, evidentiary practice in litigation is defined in large measure by the subject matter at issue. When an electric utility proposes rate changes through the regulatory process, one can reasonably expect the issues to be complex and highly technical in nature. On the other hand, resolving a question about whether a commercial motor vehicle license holder had a blood alcohol content of .04 or above may be less complex, but still dependent on technical evidence concerning the chemical analysis used in support of the charge. Even less technical or complex would be the evidence needed by an employer challenging a fired worker's claim for unemployment benefits—the employee's timecard might be all that's needed to support either side, given the right set of circumstances.

The best evidentiary practices for agency litigation, then, are defined by the character and quality of the evidence that is likely to be presented. All of the participants in the process have a role to play. The ALJ is expected to evaluate the evidence, first to determine its admissibility, and then to decide what weight to give it. For the litigator, the more complex the evidence, the greater the expectation that she will be prepared to defend its use or the grounds for its exclusion. Even the witnesses have a role here, particularly in those cases where scientific or technical evidence will be presented using expert testimony. Knowing, as we do, that many agency proceedings are not governed by state or federal rules of evidence, it's incumbent on all parties to actively anticipate evidentiary issues well in advance of the hearing and to be nimble enough to address those surprise issues that always seem to pop up in agency hearings, despite the best laid plans and preparations.

The ALJ's Duty to Marshal the Evidence and Create a Record

Housekeeping rules need to be taken into account first. Agency litigation can be notorious for having threadbare resources allocated to the gathering and preserving of evidence. The ALJ's job, of course, is to marshal the relevant evidence and preserve it. Doing so ensures the issues are determined only by evidence that is available for all to see—and not by some covert or well-hidden facts assumed to be true by the decision-maker. It also is critically important when the agency's fact-finding is scrutinized on review by appellate courts. Most reviewing courts hold the agency wholly responsible for providing a certified record of the agency's proceedings. Any material loss of evidence (such as the lack of a transcript or recording of the hearing) may be fatal to the case on appeal, nullifying the agency's action.

A Cautionary Tale—The Litigator's Duty to Create a Clear Record

The litigator, too, shares responsibility for making sure a clear record is recorded. Recall that the burden of proof is determined by identifying the proponent of the evidentiary issue in question. While the agency bears the burden of establishing a prima facie case and must prove, by at least a preponderance in most cases, each element of that case, there may still be burdens placed on responding parties. For example, a dentist had been charged with failing to properly perform root canal work on a patient, and the dental board's evidence was presented through an expert. The expert identified x-rays showing the course of treatment. He knew the minimum standards published by the board and testified that the dentist fell short by not fully clearing the root. In this way, the board met its evidentiary burden.

To respond, the dentist's attorney presented the testimony of another expert. At this stage, the burden of proof has shifted to the claimant, because the state board had met its burden of showing how the dentist failed to meet a standard set by the board. The expert was well versed in dentistry and familiar with the board's minimum standards. However, two things caused problems in his testimony. First, rather than rely on the light box used to display x-rays, he elected to project the images he reviewed using a computer and a projector. The facility we were in was not equipped with a screen, so he projected the image on a wall. He pointed out features of the root canal, assuring me that he could see evidence of root clearing, but to my eye, I could not see what he was referring to. The problem here is that a reviewing court will be unable to recreate this demonstration. The solution, I think, would have been to capture the image on paper, rather than rely on a screen projection.

The other problem in this case, and it happens frequently, is that it was exceptionally difficult to preserve what the expert was saying because he spoke too fast for the court reporter to record his testimony. He testified for nearly three hours, and both the reporter and I repeatedly admonished him to slow down, to no avail. By lunchtime, the reporter was nearly in tears, she was so frustrated by her inability to keep up with what the witness was saying. Halfway through his testimony, I explained to the witness (and to his attorney) that to the extent this testimony was needed to meet an evidentiary burden, it may fail to achieve this goal if it was presented in a way that defied accurate preservation of what he was saying.

Transcripts and Recordings

Not all hearings, we know, have court reporters. Many now are recorded by digital audio records, some still by magnetic tape, some others still by video recording. Some hearings, particularly at the national level and in jurisdictions that cover large geographical areas, are conducted with the participants in different locations. The Social Security Administration uses video conferencing for disability hearings, in which the ALJ is at her desk, and the claimant and representative are in the representative's office, all connected by audio and video transmissions. It is essential in these cases that both the ALJ and the litigators are familiar with the recording processes being used and take all necessary steps to ensure a clear, audible recording is being made.

Preparing Evidence for Admission at the Hearing

The litigator can aid the ALJ in making a clear evidentiary record. The single most useful act I've ever seen, either as an ALJ or as an agency litigator, is the practice of marking exhibits in advance of the hearing and numbering the pages in exhibits that are more than five pages long. If you will take this simple, thoughtful step, you will find the hearing progresses much smoother than it would otherwise. The second most useful step is to come to the hearing with the original of the exhibit, which you will leave with the court reporter if there is one, plus (1) a copy for the ALJ to use during the hearing and when she works on writing her decision, (2) a copy for the witness on the stand, (3) a copy for your adversary, even if you've already provided the document (unless you've provided one that is marked and paginated), and (4) a copy for yourself. The original plus four: make it a practice.

Consider Seeking a Prehearing Evidentiary and Procedural Order

As you will see, my prehearing orders always require the parties to exchange exhibits in advance of the hearing (a copy of these orders is in Appendix C and D). Your jurisdiction or your ALJ may be disinclined to use prehearing orders. I recall early in my career as a hearing examiner in Ohio, I had been appointed by the state dental board to preside over a minimum standards case. The dentist's lawyer was aggressive, and the board's assistant attorney general was equally so. My first act was to issue a prehearing order directing both sides to exchange exhibits two weeks before the hearing, and the AAG flatly refused. Now, I served as an AAG for about eight years before I became the dental board's hearing examiner, so I could appreciate the AAG's concern. At the same time, agency litigation is hard enough without there being a "trial by fire" mentality. Surprises during hearings don't benefit anyone, least of all the ALJ.

Prehearing exchanges of evidence, in my experience, permit the ALJ and the parties to focus on the truly disputed facts in issue. They also permit the alert litigant to bring to the ALJ's attention evidentiary issues that warrant prehearing discussion. Once there's a prehearing exchange of evidence, the litigant can raise objections through a motion in limine, allowing the ALJ time to give the objection some thought. Note that even in jurisdictions where there is no express provision for the filing of motions in limine, the practice is still worth pursuing. In every case I've ever seen, an ALJ who has decided to exclude factual evidence is required to permit the presenting party with the opportunity to proffer the evidence. A proffer is simply a way to place into the record a summary of the expected testimony or a copy of the disputed document. By making a written motion in limine and attaching to it the disputed document or an affidavit or summary of the expected testimony, you've created a record that can be considered by reviewing courts should you need to appeal.

Using Motions in Limine

The motion in limine works the other way as well: in addition to giving you a means by which you can insert into the record evidence that might otherwise be excluded by the ALJ, you can also use such a motion to try to prevent your opponent from introducing evidence that should be excluded. This works in much the same way as a motion to quash a subpoena. Both should be included in the agency litigator's toolbox, even where there is no express provision for them in the agency's procedural rules or in the jurisdiction's administrative procedure act. I have seen both motions used very effectively, mostly by the agency's attorney, but also in some instances by responding parties who use the motion much like a motion to suppress might be used in a criminal proceeding. Even if the motion is unsuccessful, by raising the issue in advance of the hearing, you can alert the ALJ to the points of contention so that he can review the law and consider the facts well in advance of the hearing.

Official or Administrative Notice

The taking of "official notice" or "administrative notice" is one particular instance where a prehearing motion is exceptionally useful, if not downright mandatory. Judicial-branch courts are familiar with taking "judicial notice" of the existence of facts. As Judge Toubman writes in the National Judicial College's Deskbook on Evidence for Administrative Law Judges: ALJs can be guided by Rule 201 of the Federal Rule of Evidence, which provides that "'adjudicatory' facts are those that answer what, where, when, how, and why, and are admissible if they meet a two-part test: the fact must be 'one not subject to reasonable dispute in that it is either (1) generally known within the territorial jurisdiction of the trial court or (2) capable of accurate and ready determination by resort to sources whose accuracy cannot reasonably be questioned.'"[1]

Agency proceedings, moreover, may be guided by official notice provisions that are even broader than those in the Federal Rules of Evidence. In Washington, for example, that state's administrative procedure act expressly recognizes the expertise likely to be attributed to agencies and their representatives. The statute provides that "[o]fficial notice may be taken of (a) any judicially cognizable facts, (b) technical or scientific facts within the agency's specialized knowledge, and (c) codes or standards that have been adopted by an agency of the United States, of this state or of another state, or by a nationally recognized organization or association."[2] This means that the agencies may be able to establish facts within the agency's area of expertise without necessarily presenting evidence in support of the facts. As is typically the case with such provisions, the proponent of official notice is obliged to provide notice (although not necessarily in advance of the hearing, see RCW 34.05.452(5)); and, at least in Washington, the party not offering the noticed fact "shall be afforded an opportunity to contest the facts and material so noticed."[3]

The Residuum Rule and Over-Reliance on Administrative Notice and Hearsay

In one respect, an agency's reliance on administrative or official notice has some strings attached. Case law teaches us that a case built entirely on administratively or officially noticed facts may not be constitutionally adequate. As one court stated, "to allow [the regulator] to prove his case by administrative notice is to rubber-stamp

---

1. NJC Deskbook on Evidence for Administrative Law Judges at 20 (NJC Press 2005).
2. RCW 34.05.452 (2010).
3. *Id.*

his determination."[4] Thus, if you strip away all of the administratively noticed facts, there needs to be some independent or additional evidence supporting the agency's action. This concept is known as a residuum requirement—that is, if you separate the evidence introduced through administrative notice, there must be something more supporting the government's case.

The residuum rule shows up in another evidentiary context, one concerning hearsay evidence. In some jurisdictions, hearsay alone is not enough to support a prima facie case. These jurisdictions are said to follow the residuum rule, and proceedings conducted under the rule generally require more evidence, or at least evidence less dependent on hearsay, in order for the government to meet its evidentiary burden. Consider, for example, our driver in the DUI-related case discussed earlier. Assume the arresting officer's sworn written out-of-court statement is the only evidence presented in support of a charge that the driver violated the state's implied consent law. In a state that follows the residuum rule, this would be insufficient to support a finding adverse to the driver. The Model Administrative Procedure Act does not follow the residuum rule: according to a comment, "hearsay evidence can be sufficient to support fact findings if the hearsay evidence is sufficiently reliable. This provision is based on the federal A.P.A. provision, 5 U.S.C. Section 556 (d), Richardson v. Perales, (1971) 402 U.S. 389 and the 1981 MSAPA Section 4-215(d) (reasonably prudent person standard for reliability)."[5]

Scientific and Technical Evidence, and the ALJ as Gatekeeper

Given the ubiquity and importance of technical or scientific evidence, it is important to be familiar with the "gatekeeper" role ALJs play in your jurisdiction. This follows a body of case law that arose in two decisions by the Supreme Court: *Daubert* in 1993 and *Kumho Tire Co.* in 1999. *Daubert* construes Federal Rule of Evidence 702, which concerns expert opinion based on scientific, technical, or other specialized knowledge. Under this rule, trial courts first have to determine whether the opinion would be useful in making the factual determinations necessary to the ultimate issue before the court. The judge then exercises a gatekeeper role by determining (1) whether the testimony is based on sufficient facts or data, (2) whether the testimony is the product of reliable principles and methods, and (3) whether the witness has applied the principles and methods reliably to the facts of the case.[6]

Not all jurisdictions, however, have embraced the *Daubert/Kumho* standard of evaluating expert opinion. Many retain what has come to be known as the *Frye* rule, which considers whether the theories relied on by the expert are widely accepted in

4. Lightfoot v. Mathews, 430 F. Supp. 620, 622 (N.D. Cal. 1977), quoted in NJC Deskbook on Evidence for Administrative Law Judges 23.
5. *See* Revised Model State Administrative Procedure Act, draft, section 404 Comment.
6. *See* WEINSTEIN'S FEDERAL EVIDENCE § 702.03[3] (2d ed. 2003); *see generally* NJC DESKBOOK ON EVIDENCE FOR ADMINISTRATIVE LAW JUDGES 34–40.

the relevant scientific or technical community.[7] As one court explained the different standards, "*Frye* asks judges to decide the admissibility of scientific expert testimony by deferring to the opinions of scientists in the 'pertinent field'" and requires no scientific facility in order to determine admissibility; whereas under *Daubert*, "the trial court itself is initially responsible for determining the admissibility of scientific expert testimony by determining that the science supporting that opinion is valid."[8] Thus, whenever the agency litigator anticipates the use of expert testimony that is based in scientific theory or involves technical concepts or specialized knowledge, she must determine whether her jurisdiction follows *Daubert/Kumho* or *Frye* and prepare accordingly. For a review of jurisdictions that have accepted or rejected *Daubert* in administrative proceedings, see Alice B. Luster, JD, Annotation, *Post-*Daubert *Standards for Admissibility of Scientific and Other Expert Evidence in State Courts*.[9]

Important Points

- The administrative litigator—like the ALJ—has a duty to create a clear record. If you have the burden of proof, you need to ensure all relevant evidence makes its way into the record.

- The agency has a duty to provide reviewing courts with a complete certified record. Its failure to do so may result in the court invalidating the agency's action.

- Keep the reviewing courts in mind when presenting your evidence. Be sure to make a record of gestures and other demonstrative evidence presented to the ALJ, so that it's clear what was presented during the hearing.

- You're responsible to make a clear recording wherever your client bears the burden of proof. Make sure your witnesses speak in a way that can be recorded (either by audio/video recording or by a court reporter).

- Consider retaining your own court reporter for use during the hearing.

- In advance of the hearing, mark your exhibits with letters or numbers, as directed by the ALJ. For exhibits with more than five pages, use a Bates-stamp or other sequential numbering device making it easy to turn quickly to the correct page during the hearing.

- Seek a prehearing order requiring all parties to exchange marked and paginated exhibits at least two weeks before the hearing.

- Always come to the hearing with the original exhibit and copies to give to each party, to the witness while testifying, to the court reporter, and to the ALJ (in addition to having a copy for your own use).

- Use a motion in limine to raise evidentiary issues in advance of the hearing.

---

7. Frye v. U.S., 293 F. 1013 (D.C. Cir. 1923); *see generally* NJC DESKBOOK ON EVIDENCE FOR ADMINISTRATIVE LAW JUDGES 42–43.
8. *Id.*, quoting Berry v. CSX Transp. Inc., 709 So.2d 552, 556 (Fla. Ct. App. 1998).
9. 90 A.L.R. 5th 453 (2001).

Important Points

- Be prepared for the agency's use of administrative or official notice—and know how to use such notice to support your case.

- Know whether your jurisdiction permits a finding of sufficient proof based solely on hearsay or administrative/official notice, or instead follows the residuum rule requiring more than that to support a charge.

- Know whether your jurisdiction expects the ALJ to be a gatekeeper when evaluating scientific, technical, or other specialized knowledge (the *Daubert* rule) or instead expects the ALJ to look for approval of scientific techniques in the general scientific community (the *Frye* rule); and prepare your expert examinations and cross-examinations accordingly.

CHAPTER SEVEN

COLLATERAL CHALLENGES AND THE END-RUN AROUND THE AGENCY

> Topics in this chapter include:
>
> - Theoretical Bases for Bypassing the Agency
> - Identify the Non-Administrative Issues
> - Declaratory Judgments
> - Calculate the Costs and Benefits of Bypassing the Agency
> - The First Great Writ: Mandamus
> - Prohibition
> - Procedendo
> - Habeas Corpus
> - Important Points

As we've seen, administrative agencies are invested with a blend of executive, legislative, and judicial power. To litigate successfully within administrative structures, it's important to be aware of the source of the agency's authority; and it's important to abide by procedural rules set up by the agency or by the applicable administrative procedure act. In this way, the administrative agency litigator can fully exhaust all administrative remedies—which we know is an essential prerequisite to seeking judicial review of an adverse agency decision.

There are, however, conditions under which the forum created by an agency can be bypassed, and judicial review obtained without first exhausting all administrative remedies. When properly invoked, these collateral challenges to agency action can be highly effective, particularly in the hands of an experienced civil litigator. By taking your cause directly to the judicial branch, you can dramatically alter the rules of engagement and deprive the agency of what might seem to be its home-team advantage. Most notably, by proceeding in civil court, the rules of civil procedure (and hence, discovery), apply, giving you a significant advantage over your agency— particularly in those cases where the agency's lawyer is unfamiliar with procedural and evidentiary rules used in civil trials.

Be advised that the challenges discussed below represent exceptions to the general rule that all administrative remedies must be exhausted before seeking judicial review. The general rule is well entrenched and judicial-branch courts are loath to permit the end run that skips agency litigation. It pays to keep in mind that if a civil court opens the gate, even a tiny bit, to those who otherwise would have to pursue agency remedies, then the risk of the multitudes descending on the courts becomes very real. I don't know many civil or criminal court judges who are actively looking for more business in their courts. As such, you should anticipate a skeptical reception when seeking to collaterally attack proposed agency action or make an end run around the agency.

Theoretical Bases for Bypassing the Agency

When evaluating a case to determine if agency action can be bypassed, consider first whether there is a valid legal theory permitting you to proceed to the judicial branch without exhausting administrative remedies. Recall that the theory behind delegating judicial power to agencies is based on expedience and experience. Courts defer to agencies because agencies are specialists in highly technical or high-volume governmental disputes. If you can make a strong argument that the issue involved requires none of the technical expertise of the agency, but instead requires analysis of issues that are primarily within the domain of judicial-branch courts, then you can improve your chances of presenting the issue directly to a court, bypassing the agency altogether.

Consider the hypothetical case of Dr. Tegan and Dr. Sarah, whose dental practice is being investigated by the state dental board. The board believes the two have improperly delegated certain dental services to hygienists and has issued a notice of its intention to take disciplinary action against the two dentists. This will be the first time the regulation addressing this kind of delegation of services has been raised, and the dentists maintain that the regulation is too vague to understand and should not be interpreted in the manner chosen by the board. The dentists believe, however, that the real reason for the prosecution is the fact that they maintain a Facebook page that advertises the practice as welcoming gay, lesbian, bisexual, and transgendered patients, and at least two dental board members have publicly condemned the GLBT community.

Identify the Non-Administrative Issues

The first step in the collateral attack analysis is to determine whether there's a basis for bypassing agency action altogether, and using judicial courts to stop the agency from its proposed disciplinary action. Here, the dentists may have a civil rights claim, which could be prosecuted under either state or federal equal protection laws. There is a split among courts regarding whether a claimant must exhaust administrative remedies under 42 U.S.C. 1983.[1] The general rule is that exhaustion is not required if there is no adequate remedy available through the administrative process, or where the administrative process is unduly onerous, or when the action requires resolution of constitutional issues that are beyond the expertise of the agency (which, as a practical matter, is found in all cases where the constitutionality of a statute or regulation is challenged on its face, rather than as applied).

Declaratory Judgments

Under this analysis, the dentists could seek declaratory relief in state or federal court, asserting the new dental delegation regulation is unconstitutionally vague, and invoking the civil rights protections of state or federal equal protection laws. In this way, the dentists could seek to enjoin the dental board from prosecuting the charges against them until the civil action is concluded. This permits the dentists to utilize the full range of civil discovery rights, grants them access to a judicial branch decision-maker early in the proceeding, and assures them that procedural and evidentiary rules will be those applicable in civil trials.

Calculate the Costs and Benefits of Bypassing the Agency

Before committing to such an approach, it is important to bear in mind three factors: first, seeking judicial intervention will dramatically polarize the parties and immediately garner the wrath of the regulatory body's members. Your client needs to consider the long-term impact such an adversarial tactic may have on her career. Second, this approach will likely ratchet up exponentially both the time required for resolution and the cost of litigation. And third, even where exhaustion is not required, courts still tend to abstain from resolving those issues that are highly technical or that would likely benefit from the agency's expertise.

The First Great Writ: Mandamus

Declaratory judgment actions are one way to bypass agency litigation. Four of the "great writs" provide another set of options. Mandamus, prohibition, procedendo, and habeas corpus invoke the equitable powers entrusted to our judicial branch courts and may offer a means by which agency action can be influenced, if not bypassed altogether. As is the case with declaratory judgments, proceedings conducted under the authority of these writs benefit from the application of formal evidentiary and procedural rules and generate active participation by a judicial-branch jurist early in the process.

Mandamus can be used to compel a governmental actor—be it a board, department, or individual—to act upon proof that a "clear legal duty" to perform

---

1. See, Russell J. Davis, M.A., J.D., Exhaustion of State Administrative Remedies as Prerequisite to Federal Civil Rights Action Based on 42 U.S.C.A. § 1983, 47 A.L.R. Fᴇᴅ. 15 (2010).

a public act exists, mandating that action. Again, mandamus will not be granted if there is an adequate remedy available through administrative review. There are instances, however, where (by design) no appeal is available for judicial review of final agency action. For example, Ohio's public retirement boards administratively resolve disputes over an individual worker's claim that his service made him eligible to participate in one of the state's public retirement systems. Once the board makes its determination, no appeal is available—the applicable statutes clearly provide that the board's decision is final.

To the untrained eye, that would seem to be the end of the road for the unhappy claimant. Enter mandamus: even without statutory language providing for it, an aggrieved unsuccessful individual may assert that the board has a clear legal duty to recognize the employee's work as qualifying for retirement purposes. Once the board issues its final order, the unsuccessful claimant may seek a writ of mandamus, from either the state court of appeals or its supreme court.

To be sure, mandamus technically is not an end-run around an agency's process. Mandamus is limited in scope, empowering a court only to compel an agency "to perform a ministerial or non-discretionary act," or "to take action upon a matter, without directing how it shall act."[2]   If there's an administrative forum capable of providing an adequate remedy, the forum must be used. Nevertheless, mandamus serves as an important check on agency abuse. There need be no constitutional issue involved in order to invoke the court's power in mandamus; it is sufficient to plead that the public agency or officer is under a clear legal duty to act, and has failed to act, for the writ to be granted. There need be no statute announcing the court's power to mandate governmental action—this comes from the historical power inherent in our judicial branch courts.

In addition, in some jurisdictions mandamus actions are among the rare forms of relief that can be sought—in the first instance—from appellate courts (including supreme courts). Filing an original action with the highest court in your jurisdiction is not something to be taken lightly. I've never known an appellate court to suffer fools gladly. Nevertheless, where circumstances warrant its use, mandamus can be highly effective in directly confronting an agency that is failing to perform its mandatory duties.

Prohibition

The next great writ that may prove useful in administrative litigation is the writ of prohibition. Here, a court of superior jurisdiction directs a court of inferior ju-

---

2. Norton v. S. Utah Wilderness Alliance, 542 U.S. 55, 64 (2004), quoting ATTORNEY GENERAL'S MANUAL ON THE ADMINISTRATIVE PROCEDURE ACT 108 (1947) (emphasis added), and citing L. Jaffe, JUDICIAL CONTROL OF ADMINISTRATIVE ACTION 372 (1965); K. Davis, Administrative Law § 257, 925 (1951).

risdiction to forbear action. It is designed to prevent inferior courts from exceeding their authority or usurping the role intended for another forum. When a board is engaged in fact-finding and the application of law to facts (i.e., when it's adjudicating) its conduct is regarded as quasi-judicial. A writ of prohibition may be necessary where it is shown that the board has encroached on the jurisdiction of another agency, is conducting a hearing where it lacks jurisdiction, or where its action or proposed action exceeds its jurisdiction.[3]

In practical terms, prohibition is rare, because alternative means usually exist to accomplish the same end. For example, it's not uncommon to find municipal trial courts being asked to exercise jurisdiction over appeals to driver license cases where there's an administrative process in place that needs to be exhausted first. Technically, the court has no jurisdiction over the subject matter, because jurisdiction over that issue is statutorily vested with the state licensing authority. In theory, the agency could seek a writ of prohibition—it could apply to the appellate court for a writ prohibiting the municipal court from exercising jurisdiction over the matter. In practice, the better approach is simply to file a motion with the municipal court seeking the dismissal of the action for want of jurisdiction.

Procedendo

There may be times when an inferior tribunal refuses to proceed to judgment in a case. In such instances, if the agency is acting in a quasi-judicial manner, a superior judicial tribunal may issue a writ of procedendo, directing the performance of judicial acts. Where mandamus compels the performance of ministerial acts, procedendo invokes the authority of the judicial branch to compel the executive-branch adjudicator to move forward and adjudicate, particularly where the agency is subject to time standards for action. One example of the use of actions in procedendo involves administrative claims by inmates, seeking to compel decision-making by administrative bodies charged with determining parole or property claims. The inmate may quite properly bring to the court's attention the agency's failure to timely act on his claim. The writ does not compel the agency to sustain the inmate's claim; it only requires the agency to adjudicate the claim.

Habeas Corpus

One final equitable writ that may be useful in administrative proceedings is the writ of habeas corpus. The judicial power to compel the production of a person who is under the control of the government is, as we saw in the aftermath of the attacks of September 11, 2001, a significant tool in maintaining checks and balances between the executive and judicial branches of government. Although the power of

---

3. Thompson Prods. v. NLRB, 133 F.2d 637, 639–40 (6th Cir. 1943), cited in Jacob A. Stein et al., 5 ADMINISTRATIVE LAW 46.05 (LexisNexis 2007).

the executive branch to control the physical presence of claimants is narrowly drawn (and concerns primarily issues involving immigration and enemy combatants), such

power does exist. Immigration and deportation proceedings are administrative in nature, and as such, control over the person is sometimes a factor relevant to the administrative process. Like procedendo, the writ of habeas corpus enables the judicial branch to compel decision-making, and stands as the only bulwark against the threat of unwarranted delay in executive-branch decision making. Beyond that, this writ also permits the judicial branch to address the substantive merits of the detainee's claims, at least with respect to constitutional issues.

Important Points

- The general rule is that if an administrative process exists, you must exhaust that process before resorting to the courts.

- If the issues require resolution of questions not within the scope of an agency's expertise, particularly if constitutional issues are at stake, the exhaustion doctrine may not apply.

- Any decision to try to bypass agency adjudication needs to take into account the costs and benefits of such a decision.

- Even if the court has jurisdiction and exhaustion is not required, the court may nevertheless abstain from acting until the agency has had the chance to act.

- Judicial branch courts have equitable powers that transcend and work in tandem with express powers. These include the power to grant equitable writs of mandamus, prohibition, procedendo, and habeas corpus. Agencies do not have these equitable powers.

- If the agency has a clear legal duty to act, and no appeal to the courts is provided, mandamus may be invoked to compel the agency to perform a ministerial or non-discretionary act.

- A court of superior jurisdiction has the authority to issue a writ of prohibition, enjoining an inferior court or executive tribunal from exceeding its authority or usurping the authority of another tribunal.

- Courts may also compel an inferior court or executive tribunal to go forward and adjudicate a matter, through the writ of procedendo.

- A significant feature of judicial branch courts, and a key check on executive power, is the courts' ability to compel the physical presence of persons subject to administrative process, through the writ of habeas corpus.

CHAPTER EIGHT

SETTLEMENT TOOLS: ALTERNATIVE DISPUTE RESOLUTION AND THE THREAT OF A FEE AWARD

> Topics in this chapter include:
> - Understand the Culture of Professional Courtesies
> - Good-Faith Negotiations with the Agency
> - Control Over the Government's Litigators
> - Alternative Dispute Resolution
> - Assessing the Mediators and Arbitrators Used in Administrative Agency ADR
> - Reasons to Avoid ADR
> - Attorney Fee Awards as an Inducement to Settlement
> - The Impact of Agency Structure on Attorney Fee Provisions
> - Fees from Entitlements
> - Important Points

We know that in law, as in life, information leads to knowledge, and knowledge is a form of power. Administrative agency litigation is powered by imbalances of information. If you ever want to see a governmental agency litigator light up with anger, try surprising him with last-minute documents you've held back. Discovery rules were created expressly for their ability to distribute fairly knowledge—and power—throughout the civil litigation process. As the access to discovery diminishes, so goes the equal distribution of knowledge and power.

Keeping in mind the important role information plays in agency litigation, it makes sense to employ a litigation strategy that is likely to produce the optimum array of information relevant to the issues of the case. To this end, there are carrots, and there are sticks. First, the carrots.

Understand the Culture of Professional Courtesies

Carrots in agency litigation are tactics that promote the exchange of information and produce a mutual benefit for all parties. They can be present in the form of unwritten customs, like the practice of returning phone calls within twenty-four hours; and they can be promoted through more formal means, such as procedural orders directing the exchange of information in a specific case, according to a schedule created by the ALJ, or formally published agency-wide rule concerning prehearing discovery. These are carrots because both sides benefit from the exchanges of information, in the reduced risk of surprise during the hearing, and the increased opportunity to make an informed decision about settling the case without the need of a hearing.

If this is your first appearance before the agency, take the time to learn who the key decision-makers are. Unlike private business litigation or litigation with individual parties, agency litigation is driven by concerns based on public policy. It's safe to assume the key people in the agency care deeply about acting in the public's best interest. The more you understand the policy perspectives held by those key people, the better equipped you'll be in negotiation with them. Take the time to identify the public policy that is being promoted by the regulations at play in your case—you need to know *why* the rule exists if you're going to defend your client who's accused of breaking the rule.

Good-Faith Negotiations with the Agency

As most seasoned litigators will concede, some of our clients actually did what they're accused of doing, which is to say, sometimes the government gets it right. In such cases, much can be gained by taking a careful measure of the policy priorities being advanced by the agency's key players. The agency's director may wish to obtain the maximum measure of public protection at the lowest possible cost. To do this, you may need to appeal to the agency's sense of economics by calmly explaining your intention to exercise every procedural protection and appeal if settlement terms cannot be agreed on. The agency's in-house counsel may want to protect her base by ensuring a 100 percent win record. This may signal willingness to compromise by settling through an admission that a single count of a multiple-count charge is valid in exchange for the dismissal of all other charges.

Control Over the Government's Litigators

Many agencies don't actually control their litigators. Most state attorneys general maintain a cadre of assistant attorneys general whose job is to provide litigation services to the myriad state agencies. In such cases, the litigator's first duty is to her employer, the state attorney general. Under this arrangement, the state's attorney general can be called on to reign in an agency that is over-regulating or enforcing oppressive or unreasonable regulations. In my experience, I've found significant differences in the level of commitment shown by these litigators in pursuing the policy goals of the agencies they serve. If you can demonstrate that the agency's policy goals are not supportable when examined from the broader perspective required of the state's attorney general, then you may succeed in convincing the assistant attorney general to dismiss (or nolle) the charges. Also, in those cases where the agency has an assigned litigator in addition to the in-house counsel, there may be interest in settling simply because state-wide litigation resources are stretched thin, making settlement almost imperative.

Alternative Dispute Resolution

Another highly effective resource available in some jurisdictions is a formal alternative dispute resolution program. One such program that I've encountered in many jurisdictions is the chemical or substance abuse program that permits a respondent to undergo treatment in lieu of disciplinary action. Other similar diversion-type programs are being developed as a means of addressing increased caseloads of claims that have to be processed in an environment of shrinking agency budgets.

Not all ADR programs are equal, however, and some have features that need your attention before you recommend your client's participation. Authority for federal agencies to implement ADR programs comes from 5 USC 572. Provisions in this section of the Code provide an analytical framework to use when evaluating the risk and benefits of using an alternative means of resolving your dispute with the agency. These include whether the mediator is truly neutral—is she a government employee or in some other way financially tied to the agency? Will the process be confidential? Will the outcome or supporting evidence be available for disclosure to other governmental agencies or to the public? How will any agreed-upon terms be enforced? Will there be a waiver of any right to judicial review—of the present proceeding and of any subsequent proceeding (as in prosecuting claims arising during any period of probation)?

Assessing the Mediators and Arbitrators Used in Administrative Agency ADR

Consider also impact the adjudication structure may have on the value of any ADR option. In jurisdictions where there is a highly evolved central panel of ALJs whose duties include service as mediators, you're likely to find potential mediators who are well versed in agency policy and are truly independent of the agencies—making for ideal ADR facilitators.[1] On the other hand, if the proposed mediator is a high-level administrator in the agency, the most you may gain from using the process is relatively quick and painless access to the policy-making section of the agency. This in itself can be valuable, but care should be taken not to enter into an arrangement in which the only likely outcome is a unilateral disclosure of your client's supporting evidence.

---

1. Amanda McNeil, Incorporating Alternative Dispute Resolution into State Administrative Agencies: In a Race to the Top, Which State Will Get There First? Volume 8, Issue 1, Mayhew-Hite Report on Dispute Resolution and the Courts, available at http://moritzlaw.osu.edu/jdr/ (2010).

Reasons to Avoid ADR

It also pays to understand reasons why an agency might prefer not to participate in alternative forms of resolving administrative claims. Here again, some of these reasons are presented in the federal Administrative Dispute Resolution Act.[2] An agency may shy away from pursuing an ADR outcome (1) if it believes a definitive resolution of the matter is needed to achieve the desired level of precedential value, (2) if the matter involves significant questions of governmental policy, (3) in order to maintain established policies, so as to avoid unwanted variations among individual cases, (4) if the matter significantly affects third parties who are not parties to the proceeding, (5) if a full public record is important, and (6) if circumstances warrant the agency maintaining continuing jurisdiction over the matter or the party.[3] It stands to reason that if you believe your client would be well-served by an outcome achieved through ADR, you would be wise to anticipate these factors and be prepared to demonstrate how a non-public resolution would be in the public's interest, why there's no precedential value to be gained or lost through ADR, etc.[4]

Attorney Fee Awards as an Inducement to Settlement

A mutually agreed-upon settlement, made under arms-length trading conditions, should be a positive result for all parties. When reached under fair conditions, settlement is a carrot, a worthy goal. There are, in addition, sticks that can be used to prod the government into doing the right thing by your client. First and most famous of all is the provision for an award of attorney fees in those cases where the initiation of agency action was not supported by fact or law.

At the federal level, agency proceedings conducted under the federal Administrative Procedure Act are subject to the attorney fees provisions found in the Equal Access to Justice Act of 1948. Enacted shortly after the first version of the federal Administrative Procedure Act, EAJA provides:

> [I]f the demand by the agency is substantially in excess of the decision of the adjudicative officer and is unreasonable when compared with such decision, under the facts and circumstances of the case, the adjudicative officer shall award to the party the fees and other expenses related to defending against the excessive demand, unless the party has committed a willful violation of law or otherwise acted in bad faith, or special circumstances make an award unjust.[5]

---

2. 5 USC § 571, et seq. (2006).
3. 5 USC § 572 (2006).
4. See generally, Marshall J. Breger, editor, FEDERAL ADMINISTRATIVE DISPUTE RESOLUTION DESKBOOK (ABA Publishing 2001).
5. 5 USC § 504(a)(4) (2006).

It's been my experience that hell hath no fury like an agency ordered to pay attorneys fees. This may be due, in part, to the fact that a small but distinct subgroup of attorneys who are likely to earn such awards have all the personal charm of a prickly pear. Whatever the likely reasons, agencies that are subject to such fee statutes tend to be well aware of their potential.

The Impact of Agency Structure on Attorney Fee Provisions

In some jurisdictions, attorney fees provisions are relatively toothless—particularly in those jurisdictions where the ALJ is the party charged with deciding the fee award question, and is also an employee of the agency. Here again, there is a palpable difference in cases where the ALJ is part of a central panel of administrative adjudicators and is truly independent of the agency being served. While central panel ALJs are still part of the executive branch, and they're still likely to be full-time employees of the central panel, they are insulated from agency pressure to deny awards of attorney fees. They also are in an ideal position to figuratively spank an agency for abuse and neglect in the prosecution of administrative claims.

Fees from Entitlements

There are other forms of fee provisions, beyond those that reward legal work that is needed to combat unwarranted governmental action. Many entitlement-based programs, including disability and veterans claims, provide for fees to be paid from past-due benefit awards. Generally, these provide a financial incentive to the legal community to ensure legal services are offered to deserving claimants. Factors that need to be taken into account with these fee programs include whether your legal services enhanced the prompt disposition of a favorable claim, the complexity and novelty of the issues, the amount of documentary evidence you gathered in support of the claim, and the amount of time spent on the matter.

Important Points

- Professional courtesy—returning phone calls, refraining from personal attacks—goes a long way toward fostering an environment conducive to settlement.

- Make an effort to appreciate the public policy perspectives of the agency's representatives and its policymakers.

- Remember that most public administrators strive to act in the public's best interests. It helps to frame your issues and goals in the same terms.

- With the passage of time can come a change in administrators. This can be either a blessing or a curse, depending on the personalities involved. As a result, time is a factor to keep in mind when advising your client on how best to proceed.

- Alternative dispute resolution programs exist at the federal and state levels, although the programs are neither universally available nor uniform.

Important Points
• When evaluating ADR programs, note the degree of structural independence that can be attributed to the mediator or arbitrator, and note the level of technical knowledge and expertise of those involved.
• Understand the reasons agency administrators might choose to avoid ADR, and keep them in mind when assisting your client in deciding whether to pursue ADR.
• Evaluate your client's case under any applicable attorneys' fee provisions. Knowing these provisions at the start strengthens your ability to use them as inducements to settle.

APPENDICES

Appendix A

The Federal Administrative Procedure Act
5 U.S.C. §551 et seq.

§ 551. Definitions

For the purpose of this subchapter —

(1) "agency" means each authority of the Government of the United States, whether or not it is within or subject to review by another agency, but does not include —

(A) the Congress;

(B) the courts of the United States;

(C) the governments of the territories or possessions of the United States;

(D) the government of the District of Columbia; or except as to the requirements of section 552 of this title —

(E) agencies composed of representatives of the parties or of representatives of organizations of the parties to the disputes determined by them;

(F) courts martial and military commissions;

(G) military authority exercised in the field in time of war or in occupied territory; or

(H) functions conferred by sections 1738, 1739, 1743, and 1744 of title 12; chapter 2of title 41; or sections 1622, 1884, 1891-1902, and former section 1641(b)(2), of title 50, appendix;

(2) "person" includes an individual, partnership, corporation, association, or public or private organization other than an agency;

(3) "party" includes a person or agency named or admitted as a party, or properly seeking and entitled as of right to be admitted as a party, in an agency proceeding, and a person or agency admitted by an agency as a party for limited purposes;

(4) "rule" means the whole or a part of an agency statement of general or particular applicability and future effect designed to implement, interpret, or

prescribe law or policy or describing the organization, procedure, or practice requirements of an agency and includes the approval or prescription for the future of rates, wages, corporate or financial structures or reorganizations thereof, prices, facilities, appliances, services or allowances therefore or of valuations, costs, or accounting, or practices bearing on any of the foregoing;

(5) "rule making" means agency process for formulating, amending, or repealing a rule;

(6) "order" means the whole or a part of a final disposition, whether affirmative, negative, injunctive, or declaratory in form, of an agency in a matter other than rule making but including licensing;

(7) "adjudication" means agency process for the formulation of an order;

(8) "license" includes the whole or a part of an agency permit, certificate, approval, registration, charter, membership, statutory exemption or other form of permission;

(9) "licensing" includes agency process respecting the grant, renewal, denial, revocation, suspension, annulment, withdrawal, limitation, amendment, modification, or conditioning of a license;

(10) "sanction" includes the whole or a part of an agency —

(A) prohibition, requirement, limitation, or other condition affecting the freedom of a person;

(B) withholding of relief;

(C) imposition of penalty or fine;

(D) destruction, taking, seizure, or withholding of property;

(E) assessment of damages, reimbursement, restitution, compensation, costs, charges, or fees;

(F) requirement, revocation, or suspension of a license; or

(G) taking other compulsory or restrictive action;

(11) "relief" includes the whole or a part of an agency —

(A) grant of money, assistance, license, authority, exemption, exception, privilege, or remedy;

(B) recognition of a claim, right, immunity, privilege, exemption, or exception; or

(C) taking of other action on the application or petition of, and beneficial to, a person;

(12) "agency proceeding" means an agency process as defined by paragraphs (5), (7), and (9) of this section;

(13) "agency action" includes the whole or a part of an agency rule, order, license, sanction, relief, or the equivalent or denial thereof, or failure to act; and

(14) "ex parte communication" means an oral or written communication not on the public record with respect to which reasonable prior notice to all parties is not given, but it shall not include requests for status reports on any matter or proceeding covered by this subchapter.

§ 552. Public information; agency rules, opinions, orders, records, and proceedings

(a) Each agency shall make available to the public information as follows:

(1) Each agency shall separately state and currently publish in the Federal Register for the guidance of the public—

(A) descriptions of its central and field organization and the established places at which, the employees (and in the case of a uniformed service, the members) from whom, and the methods whereby, the public may obtain information, make submittals or requests, or obtain decisions;

(B) statements of the general course and method by which its functions are channeled and determined, including the nature and requirements of all formal and informal procedures available;

(C) rules of procedure, descriptions of forms available or the places at which forms may be obtained, and instructions as to the scope and contents of all papers, reports, or examinations;

(D) substantive rules of general applicability adopted as authorized by law, and statements of general policy or interpretations of general applicability formulated and adopted by the agency; and

(E) each amendment, revision, or repeal of the foregoing.

Except to the extent that a person has actual and timely notice of the terms thereof, a person may not in any manner be required to resort to, or be adversely affected by, a matter required to be published in the Federal Register and not so published. For the purpose of this paragraph, matter reasonably available to the class of persons affected thereby is deemed published in the Federal Register when incorporated by reference therein with the approval of the Director of the Federal Register.

(2) Each agency, in accordance with published rules, shall make available for public inspection and copying—

(A) final opinions, including concurring and dissenting opinions, as well as orders, made in the adjudication of cases;

(B) those statements of policy and interpretations which have been adopted by the agency and are not published in the Federal Register;

(C) administrative staff manuals and instructions to staff that affect a member of the public;

(D) copies of all records, regardless of form or format, which have been released to any person under paragraph (3) and which, because of the nature of their subject matter, the agency determines have become or are likely to become the subject of subsequent requests for substantially the same records; and

(E) a general index of the records referred to under subparagraph (D);

unless the materials are promptly published and copies offered for sale. For records created on or after November 1, 1996, within one year after such date, each agency shall make such records available, including by computer telecommunications or, if computer telecommunications means have not been established by the agency, by other electronic means. To the extent required to prevent a clearly unwarranted invasion of personal privacy, an agency may delete identifying details when it makes available or publishes an opinion, statement of policy, interpretation, staff manual, instruction, or copies of records referred to in subparagraph (D). However, in each case the justification for the deletion shall be explained fully in writing, and the extent of such deletion shall be indicated on the portion of the record which is made available or published, unless including that indication would harm an interest protected by the exemption in subsection (b) under which the deletion is made. If technically feasible, the extent of the deletion shall be indicated at the place in the record where the deletion was made. Each agency shall also maintain and make available for public inspection and copying current indexes providing identifying information for the public as to any matter issued, adopted, or promulgated after July 4, 1967, and required by this paragraph to be made available or published. Each agency shall promptly publish, quarterly or more frequently, and distribute (by sale or otherwise) copies of each index or supplements thereto unless it determines by order published in the Federal Register that the publication would be unnecessary and impracticable, in which case the agency shall nonetheless provide copies of such index on request at a cost not to exceed the direct cost of duplication. Each agency shall make the index referred to in subparagraph (E) available by computer telecommunications by December 31, 1999. A final order, opinion, statement of policy, interpretation, or staff manual or instruction that affects a member of the public may be relied on, used, or cited as precedent by an agency against a party other than an agency only if—

(i) it has been indexed and either made available or published as provided by this paragraph; or

(ii) the party has actual and timely notice of the terms thereof.

(3)(A) Except with respect to the records made available under paragraphs (1) and (2) of this subsection, each agency, upon any request for records which (i) reasonably describes such records and (ii) is made in accordance with published rules stating the time, place, fees (if any), and procedures to be followed, shall make the records promptly available to any person.

(B) In making any record available to a person under this paragraph, an agency shall provide the record in any form or format requested by the person if the record is readily reproducible by the agency in that form or format. Each agency shall make reasonable efforts to maintain its records in forms or formats that are reproducible for purposes of this section.

(C) In responding under this paragraph to a request for records, an agency shall make reasonable efforts to search for the records in electronic form or format, except when such efforts would significantly interfere with the operation of the agency's automated information system.

(D) For purposes of this paragraph, the term "search" means to review, manually or by automated means, agency records for the purpose of locating those records which are responsive to a request.

(4)(A)(i) In order to carry out the provisions of this section, each agency shall promulgate regulations, pursuant to notice and receipt of public comment, specifying the schedule of fees applicable to the processing of requests under this section and establishing procedures and guidelines for determining when such fees should be waived or reduced. Such schedule shall conform to the guidelines which shall be promulgated, pursuant to notice and receipt of public comment, by the Director of the Office of Management and Budget and which shall provide for a uniform schedule of fees for all agencies.

(ii) Such agency regulations shall provide that—

(I) fees shall be limited to reasonable standard charges for document search, duplication, and review, when records are requested for commercial use;

(II) fees shall be limited to reasonable standard charges for document duplication when records are not sought for commercial use and the request is made by an educational or noncommercial scientific institution, whose purpose is scholarly or scientific research; or a representative of the news media; and

(III) for any request not described in (I) or (II), fees shall be limited to reasonable standard charges for document search and duplication.

(iii) Documents shall be furnished without any charge or at a charge reduced below the fees established under clause (ii) if disclosure of the information is in the public interest because it is likely to contribute significantly to public understanding of the operations or activities of the government and is not primarily in the commercial interest of the requester.

(iv) Fee schedules shall provide for the recovery of only the direct costs of search, duplication, or review. Review costs shall include only the direct costs incurred during the initial examination of a document for the purposes of determining whether the documents must be disclosed under this section and for the purposes of withholding any portions exempt from disclosure under this section. Review costs may not include any costs incurred in resolving issues of law or policy that may be raised in the course of processing a request under this section. No fee may be charged by any agency under this section—

(I) if the costs of routine collection and processing of the fee are likely to equal or exceed the amount of the fee; or

(II) for any request described in clause (ii)(II) or (III) of this subparagraph for the first two hours of search time or for the first one hundred pages of duplication.

(v) No agency may require advance payment of any fee unless the requester has previously failed to pay fees in a timely fashion, or the agency has determined that the fee will exceed $250.

(vi) Nothing in this subparagraph shall supersede fees chargeable under a statute specifically providing for setting the level of fees for particular types of records.

(vii) In any action by a requester regarding the waiver of fees under this section, the court shall determine the matter de novo: Provided, That the court's review of the matter shall be limited to the record before the agency.

(B) On complaint, the district court of the United States in the district in which the complainant resides, or has his principal place of business, or in which the agency records are situated, or in the District of Columbia, has jurisdiction to enjoin the agency from withholding agency records and to order the production of any agency records improperly withheld from the complainant. In such a case the court shall determine the matter de novo, and may examine the contents of such agency records in camera to determine whether such records or any part thereof shall be withheld under any of the exemptions set forth in subsection (b) of this section, and the burden is on the agency to sustain its action. In addition to any other matters to which a court accords substantial weight, a court shall accord substantial weight to an affidavit of an agency concerning the agency's determination as to technical feasibility under paragraph (2)(C) and subsection (b) and reproducibility under paragraph (3)(B).

(C) Notwithstanding any other provision of law, the defendant shall serve an answer or otherwise plead to any complaint made under this subsection within thirty days after service upon the defendant of the pleading in which such complaint is made, unless the court otherwise directs for good cause shown.

[(D) Repealed. Pub.L. 98-620, Title IV, § 402(2), Nov. 8, 1984, 98 Stat. 3357]

(E) The court may assess against the United States reasonable attorney fees and other litigation costs reasonably incurred in any case under this section in which the complainant has substantially prevailed.

(F) Whenever the court orders the production of any agency records improperly withheld from the complainant and assesses against the United States reasonable attorney fees and other litigation costs, and the court additionally issues a written finding that the circumstances surrounding the withholding raise questions whether agency personnel acted arbitrarily or capriciously with respect to the withholding, the Special Counsel shall promptly initiate a proceeding to determine whether disciplinary action is warranted against the officer or employee who was primarily responsible for the withholding. The Special Counsel, after investigation and consideration of the evidence submitted, shall submit his findings and recommendations to the administrative authority of the agency concerned and shall send copies of the findings and recommendations to the officer or employee or his representative. The administrative authority shall take the corrective action that the Special Counsel recommends.

(G) In the event of noncompliance with the order of the court, the district court may punish for contempt the responsible employee, and in the case of a uniformed service, the responsible member.

(5) Each agency having more than one member shall maintain and make available for public inspection a record of the final votes of each member in every agency proceeding.

(6)(A) Each agency, upon any request for records made under paragraph (1), (2), or (3) of this subsection, shall—

>   (i) determine within 20 days (excepting Saturdays, Sundays, and legal public holidays) after the receipt of any such request whether to comply with such request and shall immediately notify the person making such request of such determination and the reasons therefor, and of the right of such person to appeal to the head of the agency any adverse determination; and

>   (ii) make a determination with respect to any appeal within twenty days (excepting Saturdays, Sundays, and legal public holidays) after the receipt of such appeal. If on appeal the denial of the request for records is in whole or in part upheld, the agency shall notify the person making such request of the provisions for judicial review of that determination under paragraph (4) of this subsection.

(B)(i) In unusual circumstances as specified in this subparagraph, the time limits prescribed in either clause (i) or clause (ii) of subparagraph (A) may be extended by written notice to the person making such request setting forth the unusual circumstances for such extension and the date on which a determination is expected to be dispatched. No such notice shall specify a date that would result in an extension for more than ten working days, except as provided in clause (ii) of this subparagraph.

>   (ii) With respect to a request for which a written notice under clause (i) extends the time limits prescribed under clause (i) of subparagraph (A), the agency shall notify the person making the request if the request cannot be processed within the time limit specified in that clause and shall provide the person an opportunity to limit the scope of the request so that it may be processed within that time limit or an opportunity to arrange with the agency an alternative time frame for processing the request or a modified request. Refusal by the person to reasonably modify the request or arrange such an alternative time frame shall be

considered as a factor in determining whether exceptional circumstances exist for purposes of subparagraph (C).

(iii) As used in this subparagraph, "unusual circumstances" means, but only to the extent reasonably necessary to the proper processing of the particular requests—

(I) the need to search for and collect the requested records from field facilities or other establishments that are separate from the office processing the request;

(II) the need to search for, collect, and appropriately examine a voluminous amount of separate and distinct records which are demanded in a single request; or

(III) the need for consultation, which shall be conducted with all practicable speed, with another agency having a substantial interest in the determination of the request or among two or more components of the agency having substantial subject-matter interest therein.

(iv) Each agency may promulgate regulations, pursuant to notice and receipt of public comment, providing for the aggregation of certain requests by the same requestor, or by a group of requestors acting in concert, if the agency reasonably believes that such requests actually constitute a single request, which would otherwise satisfy the unusual circumstances specified in this subparagraph, and the requests involve clearly related matters. Multiple requests involving unrelated matters shall not be aggregated.

(C)(i) Any person making a request to any agency for records under paragraph (1), (2), or (3) of this subsection shall be deemed to have exhausted his administrative remedies with respect to such request if the agency fails to comply with the applicable time limit provisions of this paragraph. If the Government can show exceptional circumstances exist and that the agency is exercising due diligence in responding to the request, the court may retain jurisdiction and allow the agency additional time to complete its review of the records. Upon any determination by an agency to comply with a request for records, the records shall be made promptly available to such person making such request. Any notification of denial of any request for records under this subsection shall set forth the names and titles or positions of each person responsible for the denial of such request.

(ii) For purposes of this subparagraph, the term "exceptional circumstances" does not include a delay that results from a predictable agency workload of requests under this section, unless the agency demonstrates reasonable progress in reducing its backlog of pending requests.

(iii) Refusal by a person to reasonably modify the scope of a request or arrange an alternative time frame for processing a request (or a modified request) under clause (ii) after being given an opportunity to do so by the agency to whom the person made the request shall be considered as a factor in determining whether exceptional circumstances exist for purposes of this subparagraph.

(D)(i) Each agency may promulgate regulations, pursuant to notice and receipt of public comment, providing for multitrack processing of requests for records based on the amount of work or time (or both) involved in processing requests.

(ii) Regulations under this subparagraph may provide a person making a request that does not qualify for the fastest multitrack processing an opportunity to limit the scope of the request in order to qualify for faster processing.

(iii) This subparagraph shall not be considered to affect the requirement under subparagraph (C) to exercise due diligence.

(E)(i) Each agency shall promulgate regulations, pursuant to notice and receipt of public comment, providing for expedited processing of requests for records—

(I) in cases in which the person requesting the records demonstrates a compelling need; and

(II) in other cases determined by the agency.

(ii) Notwithstanding clause (i), regulations under this subparagraph must ensure—

(I) that a determination of whether to provide expedited processing shall be made, and notice of the determination shall be provided to the person making the request, within 10 days after the date of the request; and

(II) expeditious consideration of administrative appeals of such determinations of whether to provide expedited processing.

(iii) An agency shall process as soon as practicable any request for records to which the agency has granted expedited processing under this subparagraph. Agency action to deny or affirm denial of a request for expedited processing pursuant to this subparagraph, and failure by an agency to respond in a timely manner to such a request shall be subject to judicial review under paragraph (4), except that the judicial review shall be based on the record before the agency at the time of the determination.

(iv) A district court of the United States shall not have jurisdiction to review an agency denial of expedited processing of a request for records after the agency has provided a complete response to the request.

(v) For purposes of this subparagraph, the term "compelling need" means—

(I) that a failure to obtain requested records on an expedited basis under this paragraph could reasonably be expected to pose an imminent threat to the life or physical safety of an individual; or

(II) with respect to a request made by a person primarily engaged in disseminating information, urgency to inform the public concerning actual or alleged Federal Government activity.

(vi) A demonstration of a compelling need by a person making a request for expedited processing shall be made by a statement certified by such person to be true and correct to the best of such person's knowledge and belief.

(F) In denying a request for records, in whole or in part, an agency shall make a reasonable effort to estimate the volume of any requested matter the provision of which is denied, and shall provide any such estimate to the person making the request, unless providing such estimate would harm an interest protected by the exemption in subsection (b) pursuant to which the denial is made.

(b) This section does not apply to matters that are—

(1)(A) specifically authorized under criteria established by an Executive order to be kept secret in the interest of national defense or foreign policy and (B) are in fact properly classified pursuant to such Executive order;

(2) related solely to the internal personnel rules and practices of an agency;

(3) specifically exempted from disclosure by statute (other than section 552b of this title), provided that such statute (A) requires that the matters be withheld from the public in such a manner as to leave no discretion on the issue, or (B) establishes particular criteria for withholding or refers to particular types of matters to be withheld;

(4) trade secrets and commercial or financial information obtained from a person and privileged or confidential;

(5) inter-agency or intra-agency memorandums or letters which would not be available by law to a party other than an agency in litigation with the agency;

(6) personnel and medical files and similar files the disclosure of which would constitute a clearly unwarranted invasion of personal privacy;

(7) records or information compiled for law enforcement purposes, but only to the extent that the production of such law enforcement records or information (A) could reasonably be expected to interfere with enforcement proceedings, (B) would deprive a person of a right to a fair trial or an impartial adjudication, (C) could reasonably be expected to constitute an unwarranted invasion of personal privacy, (D) could reasonably be expected to disclose the identity of a confidential source, including a State, local, or foreign agency or authority or any private institution which furnished information on a confidential basis, and, in the case of a record or information compiled by criminal law enforcement authority in the course of a criminal investigation or by an agency conducting a lawful national security intelligence investigation, information furnished by a confidential source, (E) would disclose techniques and procedures for law enforcement investigations or prosecutions, or would disclose guidelines for law enforcement investigations or prosecutions if such disclosure could reasonably be expected to risk circumvention of the law, or (F) could reasonably be expected to endanger the life or physical safety of any individual;

(8) contained in or related to examination, operating, or condition reports prepared by, on behalf of, or for the use of an agency responsible for the regulation or supervision of financial institutions; or

(9) geological and geophysical information and data, including maps, concerning wells.

Any reasonably segregable portion of a record shall be provided to any person requesting such record after deletion of the portions which are exempt under this subsection. The amount of information deleted shall be indicated on the released portion of the record, unless including that indication would harm an interest protected by the exemption in this subsection under which the deletion is made. If technically feasible, the amount of the information shall be indicated at the place in the record where such deletion is made.

(c)(1) Whenever a request is made which involves access to records described in subsection (b)(7)(A) and—

(A) the investigation or proceeding involves a possible violation of criminal law; and

(B) there is reason to believe that (i) the subject of the investigation or proceeding is not aware of its pendency, and (ii) disclosure of the existence of the records could reasonably be expected to interfere with enforcement proceedings, the agency may, during only such time as that circumstance continues, treat the records as not subject to the requirements of this section.

(2) Whenever informant records maintained by a criminal law enforcement agency under an informant's name or personal identifier are requested by a third party according to the informant's name or personal identifier, the agency may treat the records as not subject to the requirements of this section unless the informant's status as an informant has been officially confirmed.

(3) Whenever a request is made which involves access to records maintained by the Federal Bureau of Investigation pertaining to foreign intelligence or counterintelligence, or international terrorism, and the existence of the records is classified information as provided in subsection (b)(1), the Bureau may, as long as the existence of the records remains classified information, treat the records as not subject to the requirements of this section.

(d) This section does not authorize withholding of information or limit the availability of records to the public, except as specifically stated in this section. This section is not authority to withhold information from Congress.

(e)(1) On or before February 1 of each year, each agency shall submit to the Attorney General of the United States a report which shall cover the preceding fiscal year and which shall include—

(A) the number of determinations made by the agency not to comply with requests for records made to such agency under subsection (a) and the reasons for each such determination;

(B)(i) the number of appeals made by persons under subsection (a)(6), the result of such appeals, and the reason for the action upon each appeal that results in a denial of information; and

(ii) a complete list of all statutes that the agency relies upon to authorize the agency to withhold information under subsection (b)(3), a description of whether a court has upheld the decision of the agency to withhold information under each such statute, and a concise description of the scope of any information withheld;

(C) the number of requests for records pending before the agency as of September 30 of the preceding year, and the median number of days that such requests had been pending before the agency as of that date;

(D) the number of requests for records received by the agency and the number of requests which the agency processed;

(E) the median number of days taken by the agency to process different types of requests;

(F) the total amount of fees collected by the agency for processing requests; and

(G) the number of full-time staff of the agency devoted to processing requests for records under this section, and the total amount expended by the agency for processing such requests.

(2) Each agency shall make each such report available to the public including by computer telecommunications, or if computer telecommunications means have not been established by the agency, by other electronic means.

(3) The Attorney General of the United States shall make each report which has been made available by electronic means available at a single electronic access point. The Attorney General of the United States shall notify the Chairman and ranking minority member of the Committee on Government Reform and Oversight of the House of Representatives and the Chairman and ranking minority member of the Committees on Governmental Affairs and the Judiciary of the Senate, no later than April 1 of the year in which each such report is issued, that such reports are available by electronic means.

(4) The Attorney General of the United States, in consultation with the Director of the Office of Management and Budget, shall develop reporting and performance guidelines in connection with reports required by this subsection by October 1, 1997, and may establish additional requirements for such reports as the Attorney General determines may be useful.

(5) The Attorney General of the United States shall submit an annual report on or before April 1 of each calendar year which shall include for the prior calendar year a listing of the number of cases arising under this section, the exemption involved in each case, the disposition of such case, and the cost, fees, and penalties assessed under subparagraphs (E), (F), and (G) of subsection (a)(4). Such report shall also include a description of the efforts undertaken by the Department of Justice to encourage agency compliance with this section.

(f) For purposes of this section, the term—

(1) "agency" as defined in section 551(1) of this title includes any executive department, military department, Government corporation, Government controlled corporation, or other establishment in the executive branch of the Government (including the Executive Office of the President), or any independent regulatory agency; and

(2) "record" and any other term used in this section in reference to information includes any information that would be an agency record subject to the requirements of this section when maintained by an agency in any format, including an electronic format.

(g) The head of each agency shall prepare and make publicly available upon request, reference material or a guide for requesting records or information from the agency, subject to the exemptions in subsection (b), including—

(1) an index of all major information systems of the agency;

(2) a description of major information and record locator systems maintained by the agency; and

(3) a handbook for obtaining various types and categories of public information from the agency pursuant to chapter 35 of title 44, and under this section.

§ 552a. Records maintained on individuals

(a) Definitions. — For purposes of this section —

(1) the term "agency" means agency as defined in section 552(e)[1]

(2) the term "individual" means a citizen of the United States or an alien lawfully admitted for permanent residence;

(3) the term "maintain" includes maintain, collect, use, or disseminate;

(4) the term "record" means any item, collection, or grouping of information about an individual that is maintained by an agency, including, but not limited to, his education, financial transactions, medical history, and criminal or employment history and that contains his name, or the identifying number, symbol, or other identifying particular assigned to the individual, such as a finger or voice print or a photograph;

(5) the term "system of records" means a group of any records under the control of any agency from which information is retrieved by the name of the indi-

---

1. Section 552(e) of this title, referred to in subsec. (a)(1), was redesignated section 552(f) of this title by section 1802(b) of Pub. L. 99-570.

vidual or by some identifying number, symbol, or other identifying particular assigned to the individual;

(6) the term "statistical record" means a record in a system of records maintained for statistical research or reporting purposes only and not used in whole or in part in making any determination about an identifiable individual, except as provided by section 8 of title 13;

(7) the term "routine use" means, with respect to the disclosure of a record, the use of such record for a purpose which is compatible with the purpose for which it was collected;

(8) the term "matching program" —

(A) means any computerized comparison of —

(i) two or more automated systems of records or a system of records with non-Federal records for the purpose of —

(I) establishing or verifying the eligibility of, or continuing compliance with statutory and regulatory requirements by, applicants for, recipients or beneficiaries of, participants in, or providers of services with respect to, cash or in-kind assistance or payments under Federal benefit programs, or

(II) recouping payments or delinquent debts under such Federal benefit programs, or

(ii) two or more automated Federal personnel or payroll systems of records or a system of Federal personnel or payroll records with non-Federal records,

(B) but does not include —

(i) matches performed to produce aggregate statistical data without any personal identifiers;

(ii) matches performed to support any research or statistical project, the specific data of which may not be used to make decisions concerning the rights, benefits, or privileges of specific individuals;

(iii) matches performed, by an agency (or component thereof) which performs as its principal function any activity pertaining to the enforcement of criminal laws, subsequent to the initiation of a specific criminal or civil law enforcement investigation of a named person or persons for the purpose of gathering evidence against such person or persons;

(iv) matches of tax information (I) pursuant to section 6103(d) of the Internal Revenue Code of 1986, (II) for purposes of tax administration as defined in section 6103(b)(4) of such Code, (III) for the purpose of intercepting a tax refund due an individual under authority granted by section 464 or 1137 of the Social Security Act; or (IV) for the purpose of intercepting a tax refund due an individual under any other tax refund intercept program authorized by statute which has been determined by the Director of the Office of Management and Budget to contain verification, notice, and hearing requirements that are substantially similar to the procedures in section 1137 of the Social Security Act;

(v) matches —

(I) using records predominantly relating to Federal personnel, that are performed for routine administrative purposes (subject to guidance provided by the Director of the Office of Management and Budget pursuant to subsection (v)); or

(II) conducted by an agency using only records from systems of records maintained by that agency; if the purpose of the match is not to take any adverse financial, personnel, disciplinary, or other adverse action against Federal personnel;

(vi) matches performed for foreign counterintelligence purposes or to produce background checks for security clearances of Federal personnel or Federal contractor personnel; or

(vii) matches performed pursuant to section 6103(l)(12) of the Internal Revenue Code of 1986 and section 1144 of the Social Security Act; or

(viii) matches performed pursuant to section 202(x)(3)or 1611(e)(1) of the Social Security Act (42 U.S.C. 402(x)(3), 1382(e)(1));

(9) the term "recipient agency" means any agency, or contractor thereof, receiving records contained in a system of records from a source agency for use in a matching program;

(10) the term "non-Federal agency" means any State or local government, or agency thereof, which receives records contained in a system of records from a source agency for use in a matching program;

(11) the term "source agency" means any agency which discloses records contained in a system of records to be used in a matching program, or any State or local government, or agency thereof, which discloses records to be used in a matching program;

(12) the term "Federal benefit program" means any program administered or funded by the Federal Government, or by any agent or State on behalf of the Federal Government, providing cash or in-kind assistance in the form of payments, grants, loans, or loan guarantees to individuals; and

(13) the term "Federal personnel" means officers and employees of the Government of the United States, members of the uniformed services (including members of the Reserve Components), individuals entitled to receive immediate or deferred retirement benefits under any retirement program of the Government of the United States (including survivor benefits).

(b) Conditions of Disclosure. — No agency shall disclose any record which is contained in a system of records by any means of communication to any person, or to another agency, except pursuant to a written request by, or with the prior written consent of, the individual to whom the record pertains, unless disclosure of the record would be —

(1) to those officers and employees of the agency which maintains the record who have a need for the record in the performance of their duties;

(2) required under section 552 of this title;

(3) for a routine use as defined in subsection (a)(7) of this section and described under subsection (e)(4)(D) of this section;

(4) to the Bureau of the Census for purposes of planning or carrying out a census or survey or related activity pursuant to the provisions of title 13;

(5) to a recipient who has provided the agency with advance adequate written assurance that the record will be used solely as a statistical research or reporting record, and the record is to be transferred in a form that is not individually identifiable;

(6) to the National Archives and Records Administration as a record which has sufficient historicalor other value to warrant its continued preservation by the United States Government, or for evaluation by the Archivist of the United States or the designee of the Archivist to determine whether the record has such value;

(7) to another agency or to an instrumentality of any governmental jurisdiction within or under the control of the United States for a civil or criminal law enforcement activity if the activity is authorized by law, and if the head of the agency or instrumentality has made a written request to the agency which maintains the record specifying the particular portion desired and the law enforcement activity for which the record is sought;

(8) to a person pursuant to a showing of compelling circumstances affecting the health or safety of an individual if upon such disclosure notification is transmitted to the last known address of such individual;

(9) to either House of Congress, or, to the extent of matter within its jurisdiction, any committee or subcommittee thereof, any joint committee of Congress or subcommittee of any such joint committee;

(10) to the Comptroller General, or any of his authorized representatives, in the course of the performance of the duties of the General Accounting Office;

(11) pursuant to the order of a court of competent jurisdiction; or

(12) to a consumer reporting agency in accordance with section 3711(f) of title 31.

(c) Accounting of Certain Disclosures. — Each agency, with respect to each system of records under its control, shall –

(1) except for disclosures made under subsections (b)(1) or (b)(2) of this section, keep an accurate accounting of —

(A) the date, nature, and purpose of each disclosure of a record to any person or to another agency made under subsection (b) of this section; and

(B) the name and address of the person or agency to whom the disclosure is made;

(2) retain the accounting made under paragraph (1) of this subsection for at least five years or the life of the record, whichever is longer, after the disclosure for which the accounting is made;

(3) except for disclosures made under subsection (b)(7) of this section, make the accounting made under paragraph (1) of this subsection available to the individual named in the record at his request; and

(4) inform any person or other agency about any correction or notation of dispute made by the agency in accordance with subsection (d) of this section of any record that has been disclosed to the person or agency if an accounting of the disclosure was made.

(d) Access to Records. — Each agency that maintains a system of records shall —

(1) upon request by any individual to gain access to his record or to any information pertaining to him which is contained in the system, permit him and upon his request, a person of his own choosing to accompany him, to review the record and have a copy made of all or any portion thereof in a form comprehensible to him, except that the agency may require the individual to furnish

a written statement authorizing discussion of that individual's record in the accompanying person's presence;

(2) permit the individual to request amendment of a record pertaining to him and —

(A) not later than 10 days (excluding Saturdays, Sundays, and legal public holidays) after the date of receipt of such request, acknowledge in writing such receipt; and

(B) promptly, either —

(i) make any correction of any portion thereof which the individual believes is not accurate, relevant, timely, or complete; or

(ii) inform the individual of its refusal to amend the record in accordance with his request, the reason for the refusal, the procedures established by the agency for the individual to request a review of that refusal by the head of the agency or an officer designated by the head of the agency, and the name and business address of that official;

(3) permit the individual who disagrees with the refusal of the agency to amend his record to request a review of such refusal, and not later than 30 days (excluding Saturdays, Sundays, and legal public holidays) from the date on which the individual requests such review, complete such review and make a final determination unless, for good cause shown, the head of the agency extends such 30-day period; and if, after his review, the reviewing official also refuses to amend the record in accordance with the request, permit the individual to file with the agency a concise statement setting forth the reasons for his disagreement with the refusal of the agency, and notify the individual of the provisions for judicial review of the reviewing official's determination under subsection (g)(1)(A) of this section;

(4) in any disclosure, containing information about which the individual has filed a statement of disagreement, occurring after the filing of the statement under paragraph (3) of this subsection, clearly note any portion of the record which is disputed and provide copies of the statement and, if the agency deems it appropriate, copies of a concise statement of the reasons of the agency for not making the amendments requested, to persons or other agencies to whom the disputed record has been disclosed; and

(5) nothing in this section shall allow an individual access to any information compiled in reasonable anticipation of a civil action or proceeding.

(e) Agency Requirements. — Each agency that maintains a system of records shall —

(1) maintain in its records only such information about an individual as is relevant and necessary to accomplish a purpose of the agency required to be accomplished by statute or by executive order of the President;

(2) collect information to the greatest extent practicable directly from the subject individual when the information may result in adverse determinations about an individual's rights, benefits, and privileges under Federal programs;

(3) inform each individual whom it asks to supply information, on the form which it uses to collect the information or on a separate form that can be retained by the individual —

(A) the authority (whether granted by statute, or by executive order of the President) which authorizes the solicitation of the information and whether disclosure of such information is mandatory or voluntary;

(B) the principal purpose or purposes for which the information is intended to be used;

(C) the routine uses which may be made of the information, as published pursuant to paragraph (4)(D) of this subsection; and

(D) the effects on him, if any, of not providing all or any part of the requested information;

(4) subject to the provisions of paragraph (11) of this subsection, publish in the Federal Register upon establishment or revision a notice of the existence and character of the system of records, which notice shall include —

(A) the name and location of the system;

(B) the categories of individuals on whom records are maintained in the system;

(C) the categories of records maintained in the system;

(D) each routine use of the records contained in the system, including the categories of users and the purpose of such use;

(E) the policies and practices of the agency regarding storage, retrievability, access controls, retention, and disposal of the records;

(F) the title and business address of the agency official who is responsible for the system of records;

(G) the agency procedures whereby an individual can be notified at his request if the system of records contains a record pertaining to him;

(H) the agency procedures whereby an individual can be notified at his request how he can gain access to any record pertaining to him contained in the system of records, and how he can contest its content; and

(I) the categories of sources of records in the system;

(5) maintain all records which are used by the agency in making any determination about any individual with such accuracy, relevance, timeliness, and completeness as is reasonably necessary to assure fairness to the individual in the determination;

(6) prior to disseminating any record about an individual to any person other than an agency, unless the dissemination is made pursuant to subsection (b)(2) of this section, make reasonable efforts to assure that such records are accurate, complete, timely, and relevant for agency purposes;

(7) maintain no record describing how any individual exercises rights guaranteed by the First Amendment unless expressly authorized by statute or by the individual about whom the record is maintained or unless pertinent to and within the scope of an authorized law enforcement activity;

(8) make reasonable efforts to serve notice on an individual when any record on such individual is made available to any person under compulsory legal process when such process becomes a matter of public record;

(9) establish rules of conduct for persons involved in the design, development, operation, or maintenance of any system of records, or in maintaining any record, and instruct each such person with respect to such rules and the requirements of this section, including any other rules and procedures adopted pursuant to this section and the penalties for noncompliance;

(10) establish appropriate administrative, technical, and physical safeguards to insure the security and confidentiality of records and to protect against any anticipated threats or hazards to their security or integrity which could result in substantial harm, embarrassment, inconvenience, or unfairness to any individual on whom information is maintained;

(11) at least 30 days prior to publication of information under paragraph (4) (D) of this subsection, publish in the Federal Register notice of any new use or intended use of the information in the system, and provide an opportunity for interested persons to submit written data, views, or arguments to the agency; and

(12) if such agency is a recipient agency or a source agency in a matching program with a non-Federal agency, with respect to any establishment or revision

of a matching program, at least 30 days prior to conducting such program, publish in the Federal Register notice of such establishment or revision.

(f) Agency Rules. — In order to carry out the provisions of this section, each agency that maintains a system of records shall promulgate rules, in accordance with the requirements (including general notice) of section 553 of this title, which shall —

(1) establish procedures whereby an individual can be notified in response to his request if any system of records named by the individual contains a record pertaining to him;

(2) define reasonable times, places, and requirements for identifying an individual who requests his record or information pertaining to him before the agency shall make the record or information available to the individual;

(3) establish procedures for the disclosure to an individual upon his request of his record or information pertaining to him, including special procedure, if deemed necessary, for the disclosure to an individual of medical records, including psychological records, pertaining to him;

(4) establish procedures for reviewing a request from an individual concerning the amendment of any record or information pertaining to the individual, for making a determination on the request, for an appeal within the agency of an initial adverse agency determination, and for whatever additional means may be necessary for each individual to be able to exercise fully his rights under this section; and

(5) establish fees to be charged, if any, to any individual for making copies of his record, excluding the cost of any search for and review of the record. The Office of the Federal Register shall biennially compile and publish the rules promulgated under this subsection and agency notices published under subsection (e) (4) of this section in a form available to the public at low cost.

(g)(1) Civil Remedies. — Whenever any agency

(A) makes a determination under subsection (d)(3) of this section not to amend an individual's record in accordance with his request, or fails to make such review in conformity with that subsection;

(B) refuses to comply with an individual request under subsection (d)(1) of this section;

(C) fails to maintain any record concerning any individual with such accuracy, relevance, timeliness, and completeness as is necessary to assure fairness in any determination relating to the qualifications, character, rights, or opportunities of, or benefits to the individual that may be made on the basis of such record, and consequently a determination is made which is adverse to the individual; or

(D) fails to comply with any other provision of this section, or any rule promulgated thereunder, in such a way as to have an adverse effect on an individual, the individual may bring a civil action against the agency, and the district courts of the United States shall have jurisdiction in the matters under the provisions of this subsection.

(2)(A) In any suit brought under the provisions of subsection (g)(1)(A) of this section, the court may order the agency to amend the individual's record in accordance with his request or in such other way as the court may direct. In such a case the court shall determine the matter de novo.

(B) The court may assess against the United States reasonable attorney fees and other litigation costs reasonably incurred in any case under this paragraph in which the complainant has substantially prevailed.

(3)(A) In any suit brought under the provisions of subsection (g)(1)(B) of this section, the court may enjoin the agency from withholding the records and order the production to the complainant of any agency records improperly withheld from him. In such a case the court shall determine the matter de novo, and may examine the contents of any agency records in camera to determine whether the records or any portion thereof may be withheld under any of the exemptions set forth in subsection (k) of this section, and the burden is on the agency to sustain its action.

(B) The court may assess against the United States reasonable attorney fees and other litigation costs reasonably incurred in any case under this paragraph in which the complainant has substantially prevailed.

(4) In any suit brought under the provisions of subsection (g)(1)(C) or (D) of this section in which the court determines that the agency acted in a manner which was intentional or willful, the United States shall be liable to the individual in an amount equal to the sum of —

(A) actual damages sustained by the individual as a result of the refusal or failure, but in no case shall a person entitled to recovery receive less than the sum of $1,000; and

(B) the costs of the action together with reasonable attorney fees as determined by the court.

(5) An action to enforce any liability created under this section may be brought in the district court of the United States in the district in which the complainant resides, or has his principal place of business, or in which the agency records

are situated, or in the District of Columbia, without regard to the amount in controversy, within two years from the date on which the cause of action arises, except that where an agency has materially and willfully misrepresented any information required under this section to be disclosed to an individual and the information so misrepresented is material to establishment of the liability of the agency to the individual under this section, the action may be brought at any time within two years after discovery by the individual of the misrepresentation. Nothing in this section shall be construed to authorize any civil action by reason of any injury sustained as the result of a disclosure of a record prior to September 27, 1975.

(h) Rights of Legal Guardians. — For the purposes of this section, the parent of any minor, or the legal guardian of any individual who has been declared to be incompetent due to physical or mental incapacity or age by a court of competent jurisdiction, may act on behalf of the individual.

(i)(1) Criminal Penalties. — Any officer or employee of an agency, who by virtue of his employment or official position, has possession of, or access to, agency records which contain individually identifiable information the disclosure of which is prohibited by this section or by rules or regulations established thereunder, and who knowing that disclosure of the specific material is so prohibited, willfully discloses the material in any manner to any person or agency not entitled to receive it, shall be guilty of a misdemeanor and fined not more than $5,000.

(2) Any officer or employee of any agency who willfully maintains a system of records without meeting the notice requirements of subsection (e)(4) of this section shall be guilty of a misdemeanor and fined not more than $5,000.

(3) Any person who knowingly and willfully requests or obtains any record concerning an individual from an agency under false pretenses shall be guilty of a misdemeanor and fined not more than $5,000.

(j) General Exemptions. — The head of any agency may promulgate rules, in accordance with the requirements (including general notice) of sections 553(b)(1), (2), and (3), (c), and (e) of this title, to exempt any system of records within the agency from any part of this section except subsections (b), (c)(1) and (2), (e)(4) (A) through (F), (e)(6), (7), (9), (10), and (11), and (i) if the system of records is —

(1) maintained by the Central Intelligence Agency; or

(2) maintained by an agency or component thereof which performs as its principal function any activity pertaining to the enforcement of criminal laws, including police efforts to prevent, control, or reduce crime or to apprehend criminals, and the activities of prosecutors, courts, correctional, probation, pardon, or parole authorities, and which consists of (A)information compiled for

the purpose of identifying individual criminal offenders and alleged offenders and consisting only of identifying data and notations of arrests, the nature and disposition of criminal charges, sentencing, confinement, release, and parole and probation status;(B) information compiled for the purpose of a criminal investigation, including reports of informants and investigators, and associated with an identifiable individual; or (C) reports identifiable to an individual compiled at any stage of the process of enforcement of the criminal laws from arrest or indictment through release from supervision.

At the time rules are adopted under this subsection, the agency shall include in the statement required under section 553(c) of this title, the reasons why the system of records is to be exempted from a provision of this section.

(k) Specific Exemptions. — The head of any agency may promulgate rules, in accordance with the requirements (including general notice) of sections 553(b)(1), (2), and (3), (c), and (e) of this title, to exempt any system of records within the agency from subsections (c)(3), (d), (e)(1), (e)(4)(G), (H), and (I) and (f) of this section if the system of records is –

(1) subject to the provisions of section 552(b)(1) of this title;

(2) investigatory material compiled for law enforcement purposes, other than material within the scope of subsection (j)(2) of this section: Provided, however, That if any individual is denied any right, privilege, or benefit that he would otherwise be entitled by Federal law, or for which he would otherwise be eligible, as a result of the maintenance of such material, such material shall be provided to such individual, except to the extent that the disclosure of such material would reveal the identity of a source who furnished information to the Government under an express promise that the identity of the source would be held in confidence, or, prior to the effective date of this section, under an implied promise that the identity of the source would be held in confidence;

(3) maintained in connection with providing protective services to the President of the United States or other individuals pursuant to section 3056 of title 18;

(4) required by statute to be maintained and used solely as statistical records;

(5) investigatory material compiled solely for the purpose of determining suitability, eligibility, or qualifications for Federal civilian employment, military service, Federal contracts, or access to classified information, but only to the extent that the disclosure of such material would reveal the identity of a source who furnished information to the Government under an express promise that the identity of the source would be held in confidence, or, prior to the effective date of this section, under an implied promise that the identity of the source would be held in confidence;

(6) testing or examination material used solely to determine individual qualifications for appointment or promotion in the Federal service the disclosure of which would compromise the objectivity or fairness of the testing or examination process; or

(7) evaluation material used to determine potential for promotion in the armed services, but only to the extent that the disclosure of such material would reveal the identity of a source who furnished information to the Government under an express promise that the identity of the source would be held in confidence, or, prior to the effective date of this section, under an implied promise that the identity of the source would be held in confidence.

At the time rules are adopted under this subsection, the agency shall include in the statement required under section 553(c) of this title, the reasons why the system of records is to be exempted from a provision of this section.

(*l*)(1) Archival Records. — Each agency record which is accepted by the Archivist of the United States for storage, processing, and servicing in accordance with section 3103 of title 44 shall, for the purposes of this section, be considered to be maintained by the agency which deposited the record and shall be subject to the provisions of this section. The Archivist of the United States shall not disclose the record except to the agency which maintains the record, or under rules established by that agency which are not inconsistent with the provisions of this section.

(2) Each agency record pertaining to an identifiable individual which was transferred to the National Archives of the United States as a record which has sufficient historical or other value to warrant its continued preservation by the United States Government, prior to the effective date of this section, shall, for the purposes of this section, be considered to be maintained by the National Archives and shall not be subject to the provisions of this section, except that a statement generally describing such records (modeled after the requirements relating to records subject to subsections (e)(4)(A) through (G) of this section) shall be published in the Federal Register.

(3) Each agency record pertaining to an identifiable individual which is transferred to the National Archives of the United States as a record which has sufficient historical or other value to warrant its continued preservation by the United States Government, on or after the effective date of this section, shall, for the purposes of this section, be considered to be maintained by the National Archives and shall be exempt from the requirements of this section except subsections (e)(4)(A) through (G) and (e)(9) of this section.

(m)(1) Government Contractors. — When an agency provides by a contract for the operation by or on behalf of the agency of a system of records to accomplish an agency function, the agency shall, consistent with its authority, cause the requirements of this section to be applied to such system. For purposes of subsection (i) of this section any such contractor and any employee of such contractor, if such contract is agreed to on or after the effective date of this section, shall be considered to be an employee of an agency.

(2) A consumer reporting agency to which a record is disclosed under section 3711(f) of title 31 shall not be considered a contractor for the purposes of this section.

(n) Mailing Lists. — An individual's name and address may not be sold or rented by an agency unless such action is specifically authorized by law. This provision shall not be construed to require the withholding of names and addresses otherwise permitted to be made public.

(o) Matching Agreements. — (1) No record which is contained in a system of records may be disclosed to a recipient agency or non-Federal agency for use in a computer matching program except pursuant to a written agreement between the source agency and the recipient agency or non-Federal agency specifying —

(A) the purpose and legal authority for conducting the program;

(B) the justification for the program and the anticipated results, including a specific estimate of any savings;

(C) a description of the records that will be matched, including each data element that will be used, the approximate number of records that will be matched, and the projected starting and completion dates of the matching program;

(D) procedures for providing individualized notice at the time of application, and notice periodically thereafter as directed by the Data Integrity Board of such agency (subject to guidance provided by the Director of the Office of Management and Budget pursuant to subsection (v)), to —

(i) applicants for and recipients of financial assistance or payments under Federal benefit programs, and

(ii) applicants for and holders of positions as Federal personnel, that any information provided by such applicants, recipients, holders, and individuals may be subject to verification through matching programs;

(E) procedures for verifying information produced in such matching program as required by subsection (p);

(F) procedures for the retention and timely destruction of identifiable records created by a recipient agency or non-Federal agency in such matching program;

(G) procedures for ensuring the administrative, technical, and physical security of the records matched and the results of such programs;

(H) prohibitions on duplication and redisclosure of records provided by the source agency within or outside the recipient agency or the non-Federal agency, except where required by law or essential to the conduct of the matching program;

(I) procedures governing the use by a recipient agency or non-Federal agency of records provided in a matching program by a source agency, including procedures governing return of the records to the source agency or destruction of records used in such program;

(J) information on assessments that have been made on the accuracy of the records that will be used in such matching program; and

(K) that the Comptroller General may have access to all records of a recipient agency or a non-Federal agency that the Comptroller General deems necessary in order to monitor or verify compliance with the agreement.

(2)(A) A copy of each agreement entered into pursuant to paragraph (1) shall —

(i) be transmitted to the Committee on Governmental Affairs of the Senate and the Committee on Government Operations of the House of Representatives; and

(ii) be available upon request to the public.

(B) No such agreement shall be effective until 30 days after the date on which such a copy is transmitted pursuant to subparagraph (A)(i).

(C) Such an agreement shall remain in effect only for such period, not to exceed 18 months, as the Data Integrity Board of the agency determines is appropriate in light of the purposes, and length of time necessary for the conduct, of the matching program.

(D) Within 3 months prior to the expiration of such an agreement pursuant to subparagraph (C), the Data Integrity Board of the agency may, without additional review, renew the matching agreement for a current, ongoing matching program for not more than one additional year if —

(i) such program will be conducted without any change; and

(ii) each party to the agreement certifies to the Board in writing that the program has been conducted in compliance with the agreement.

(p) Verification and Opportunity to Contest Findings. — (1) In order to protect any individual whose records are used in a matching program, no recipient agency, non-Federal agency, or source agency may suspend, terminate, reduce, or make a final denial of any financial assistance or payment under a Federal benefit program to such individual, or take other adverse action against such individual, as a result of information produced by such matching program, until —

(A)(i) the agency has independently verified the information; or

(ii) the Data Integrity Board of the agency, or in the case of a non-Federal agency the Data Integrity Board of the source agency, determines in accordance with guidance issued by the Director of the Office of Management and Budget that —

(I) the information is limited to identification and amount of benefits paid by the source agency under a Federal benefit program; and

(II) there is a high degree of confidence that the information provided to the recipient agency is accurate;

(B) the individual receives a notice from the agency containing a statement of its findings and informing the individual of the opportunity to contest such findings; and

(C)(i) the expiration of any time period established for the program by statute or regulation for the individual to respond to that notice; or

(ii) in the case of a program for which no such period is established, the end of the 30-day period beginning on the date on which notice under subparagraph (B) is mailed or otherwise provided to the individual.

(2) Independent verification referred to in paragraph (1) requires investigation and confirmation of specific information relating to an individual that is used as a basis for an adverse action against the individual, including where applicable investigation and confirmation of —

(A) the amount of any asset or income involved;

(B) whether such individual actually has or had access to such asset or income for such individual's own use; and

(C) the period or periods when the individual actually had such asset or income.

(3) Notwithstanding paragraph (1), an agency may take any appropriate action otherwise prohibited by such paragraph if the agency determines that the public health or public safety may be adversely affected or significantly threatened during any notice period required by such paragraph.

(q) Sanctions. — (1) Notwithstanding any other provision of law, no source agency may disclose any record which is contained in a system of records to a recipient agency or non-Federal agency or a matching program if such source agency has reason to believe that the requirements of subsection

(p), or any matching agreement entered into pursuant to subsection (o), or both, are not being met by such recipient agency.

(2) No source agency may renew a matching agreement unless —

(A) the recipient agency or non-Federal agency has certified that it has complied with the provisions of that agreement; and

(B) the source agency has no reason to believe that the certification is inaccurate.

(r) Report on New Systems and Matching Programs. — Each agency that proposes to establish or make a significant change in a system of records or a matching program shall provide adequate advance notice of any such proposal (in duplicate) to the Committee on Government Operations of the House of Representatives, the Committee on Governmental Affairs of the Senate, and the Office of Management and Budget in order to permit an evaluation of the probable or potential effect of such proposal on the privacy or other rights of individuals.

(s) Biennial Report. — The President shall biennially submit to the Speaker of the House of Representatives and the President pro tempore of the Senate a report —

(1) describing the actions of the Director of the Office of Management and Budget pursuant to section 6 of the Privacy Act of 1974 during the preceding 2 years;

(2) describing the exercise of individual rights of access and amendment under this section during such years;

(3) identifying changes in or additions to systems of records;

(4) containing such other information concerning administration of this section as may be necessary or useful to the Congress in reviewing the effectiveness of this section in carrying out the purposes of the Privacy Act of 1974.

(t)(1) Effect of Other Laws. — No agency shall rely on any exemption contained in section 552 of this title to withhold from an individual any record which is otherwise accessible to such individual under the provisions of this section.

(2) No agency shall rely on any exemption in this section to withhold from an individual any record which is otherwise accessible to such individual under the provisions of section 552 of this title.

(u) Data Integrity Boards. — (1) Every agency conducting or participating in a matching program shall establish a Data Integrity Board to oversee and coordinate among the various components of such agency the agency's implementation of this section.

(2) Each Data Integrity Board shall consist of senior officials designated by the head of the agency, and shall include any senior official designated by the head of the agency as responsible for implementation of this section, and the inspector general of the agency, if any. The inspector general shall not serve as chairman of the Data Integrity Board.

(3) Each Data Integrity Board —

(A) shall review, approve, and maintain all written agreements for receipt or disclosure of agency records for matching programs to ensure compliance with subsection (o), and all relevant statutes, regulations, and guidelines;

(B) shall review all matching programs in which the agency has participated during the year, either as a source agency or recipient agency, determine compliance with applicable laws, regulations, guidelines, and agency agreements, and assess the costs and benefits of such programs;

(C) shall review all recurring matching programs in which the agency has participated during the year, either as a source agency or recipient agency, for continued justification for such disclosures;

(D) shall compile an annual report, which shall be submitted to the head of the agency and the Office of Management and Budget and made available to the public on request, describing the matching activities of the agency, including —

(i) matching programs in which the agency has participated as a source agency or recipient agency;

(ii) matching agreements proposed under subsection (o) that were disapproved by the Board;

(iii) any changes in membership or structure of the Board in the preceding year;

(iv) the reasons for any waiver of the requirement in paragraph (4) of this section for completion and submission of a cost-benefit analysis prior to the approval of a matching program;

(v) any violations of matching agreements that have been alleged or identified and any corrective action taken; and

(vi) any other information required by the Director of the Office of Management and Budget to be included in such report;

(E) shall serve as a clearinghouse for receiving and providing information on the accuracy, completeness, and reliability of records used in matching programs;

(F) shall provide interpretation and guidance to agency components and personnel on the requirements of this section for matching programs;

(G) shall review agency recordkeeping and disposal policies and practices for matching programs to assure compliance with this section; and

(H) may review and report on any agency matching activities that are not matching programs.

(4)(A) Except as provided in subparagraphs (B) and (C), a Data Integrity Board shall not approve any written agreement for a matching program unless the agency has completed and submitted to such Board a cost-benefit analysis of the proposed program and such analysis demonstrates that the program is likely to be cost effective.[2]

(B) The Board may waive the requirements of subparagraph (A) of this paragraph if it determines in writing, in accordance with guidelines prescribed by the Director of the Office of Management and Budget, that a cost-benefit analysis is not required.

(C) A cost-benefit analysis shall not be required under subparagraph (A) prior to the initial approval of a written agreement for a matching program that is specifically required by statute. Any subsequent written agreement for such a program shall not be approved by the Data Integrity Board unless the agency has submitted a cost-benefit analysis of the program as conducted under the preceding approval of such agreement.

(5)(A) If a matching agreement is disapproved by a Data Integrity Board, any party to such agreement may appeal the disapproval to the Director of the Of-

---

2. So in original. Probably should be "cost-effective."

fice of Management and Budget. Timely notice of the filing of such an appeal shall be provided by the Director of the Office of Management and Budget to the Committee on Governmental Affairs of the Senate and the Committee on Government Operations of the House of Representatives.

(B) The Director of the Office of Management and Budget may approve a matching agreement notwithstanding the disapproval of a Data Integrity Board if the Director determines that —

(i) the matching program will be consistent with all applicable legal, regulatory, and policy requirements;

(ii) there is adequate evidence that the matching agreement will be cost-effective; and

(iii) the matching program is in the public interest.

(C) The decision of the Director to approve a matching agreement shall not take effect until 30 days after it is reported to committees described in subparagraph (A).

(D) If the Data Integrity Board and the Director of the Office of Management and Budget disapprove a matching program proposed by the inspector general of an agency, the inspector general may report the disapproval to the head of the agency and to the Congress.

(6) In the reports required by paragraph (3)(D), agency matching activities that are not matching programs may be reported on an aggregate basis, if and to the extent necessary to protect ongoing law enforcement or counterintelligence investigations.

(v) Office of Management and Budget Responsibilities. — The Director of the Office of Management and Budget shall —

(1) develop and, after notice and opportunity for public comment, prescribe guidelines and regulations for the use of agencies in implementing the provisions of this section; and

(2) provide continuing assistance to and oversight of the implementation of this section by agencies.

§ 552b. Open meetings

(a) For purposes of this section —

(1) the term "agency" means any agency, as defined in section 552(e)[3] of this title, headed by a collegial body composed of two or more individual members,

---

3. Section 552(e) of this title, referred to in subsec. (a)(1), was redesignated section 552(f) of this title

a majority of whom are appointed to such position by the President with the advice and consent of the Senate, and any subdivision thereof authorized to act on behalf of the agency;

(2) the term "meeting" means the deliberations of at least the number of individual agency members required to take action on behalf of the agency where such deliberations determine or result in the joint conduct or disposition of official agency business, but does not include deliberations required or permitted by subsection (d) or (e); and

(3) the term "member" means an individual who belongs to a collegial body heading an agency.

(b) Members shall not jointly conduct or dispose of agency business other than in accordance with this section. Except as provided in subsection (c), every portion of every meeting of an agency shall be open to public observation. (c) Except in a case where the agency finds that the public interest requires otherwise, the second sentence of subsection (b) shall not apply to any portion of an agency meeting, and the requirements of subsections (d) and (e) shall not apply to any information pertaining to such meeting otherwise required by this section to be disclosed to the public, where the agency properly determines that such portion or portions of its meeting or the disclosure of such information is likely to —

(1) disclose matters that are (A) specifically authorized under criteria established by an Executive order to be kept secret in the interests of national defense or foreign policy and (B) in fact properly classified pursuant to such Executive order;

(2) relate solely to the internal personnel rules and practices of an agency;

(3) disclose matters specifically exempted from disclosure by statute (other than section 552 of this title), provided that such statute (A) requires that the matters be withheld from the public in such a manner as to leave no discretion on the issue, or (B) establishes particular criteria for withholding or refers to particular types of matters to be withheld;

(4) disclose trade secrets and commercial or financial information obtained from a person and privileged or confidential;

(5) involve accusing any person of a crime, or formally censuring any person;

(6) disclose information of a personal nature where disclosure would constitute a clearly unwarranted invasion of personal privacy;

---

by section 1802(b) of Pub. L. 99-570.

(7) disclose investigatory records compiled for law enforcement purposes, or information which if written would be contained in such records, but only to the extent that the production of such records or information would (A) interfere with enforcement proceedings, (B) deprive a person of a right to a fair trial or an impartial adjudication, (C) constitute an unwarranted invasion of personal privacy, (D) disclose the identity of a confidential source and, in the case of a record compiled by a criminal law enforcement authority in the course of a criminal investigation, or by an agency conducting a lawful national security intelligence investigation, confidential information furnished only by the confidential source, (E) disclose investigative techniques and procedures, or (F) endanger the life or physical safety of law enforcement personnel;

(8) disclose information contained in or related to examination, operating, or condition reports prepared by, on behalf of, or for the use of an agency responsible for the regulation or supervision of financial institutions;

(9) disclose information the premature disclosure of which would —

(A) in the case of an agency which regulates currencies, securities, commodities, or financial institutions, be likely to (i) lead to significant financial speculation in currencies, securities, or commodities, or (ii) significantly endanger the stability of any financial institution; or

(B) in the case of any agency, be likely to significantly frustrate implementation of a proposed agency action, that subparagraph (B) shall not apply in any instance where the agency has already disclosed to the public the content or nature of its proposed action, or where the agency is required by law to make such disclosure on its own initiative prior to taking final agency action on such proposal; or

(10) specifically concern the agency's issuance of a subpena [sic], or the agency's participation in a civil action or proceeding, an action in a foreign court or international tribunal, or an arbitration, or the initiation, conduct, or disposition by the agency of a particular case of formal agency adjudication pursuant to the procedures in section 554 of this title or otherwise involving a determination on the record after opportunity for a hearing.

(d)(1) Action under subsection (c) shall be taken only when a majority of the entire membership of the agency (as defined in subsection (a)(1)) votes to take such action. A separate vote of the agency members shall be taken with respect to each agency meeting a portion or portions of which are proposed to be closed to the public pursuant to subsection (c), or with respect to any information which is proposed to be withheld under subsection (c). A single vote may be taken with respect to a series of meetings, a portion or portions of which are proposed to be closed to the public, or with respect to any information concerning such series of meetings, so long as each meeting in such series involves the same particular matters and is scheduled to be held no more than thirty days after the initial meeting in such series. The vote of each agency member participating in such vote shall be recorded and no proxies shall be allowed.

(2) Whenever any person whose interests may be directly affected by a portion of a meeting requests that the agency close such portion to the public for any of the reasons referred to in paragraph (5), (6), or (7) of subsection (c), the agency, upon request of any one of its members, shall vote by recorded vote whether to close such meeting.

(3) Within one day of any vote taken pursuant to paragraph (1) or (2), the agency shall make publicly available a written copy of such vote reflecting the vote of each member on the question. If a portion of a meeting is to be closed to the public, the agency shall, within one day of the vote taken pursuant to paragraph (1) or (2) of this subsection, make publicly available a full written explanation of its action closing the portion together with a list of all persons expected to attend the meeting and their affiliation.

(4) Any agency, a majority of whose meetings may properly be closed to the public pursuant to paragraph (4), (8), (9)(A), or (10) of subsection (c), or any combination thereof, may provide by regulation for the closing of such meetings or portions thereof in the event that a majority of the members of the agency votes by recorded vote at the beginning of such meeting, or portion thereof, to close the exempt portion or portions of the meeting, and a copy of such vote, reflecting the vote of each member on the question, is made available to the public. The provisions of paragraphs (1), (2), and (3) of this subsection and subsection (e) shall not apply to any portion of a meeting to which such regulations apply: Provided, That the agency shall, except to the extent that such information is exempt from disclosure under the provisions of subsection (c), provide the public with public announcement of the time, place, and subject matter of the meeting and of each portion thereof at the earliest practicable time.

(e)(1) In the case of each meeting, the agency shall make public announcement, at least one week before the meeting, of the time, place, and subject matter of the meeting, whether it is to be open or closed to the public, and the name and phone number of the official designated by the agency to respond to requests for information about the meeting. Such announcement shall be made unless a majority of the members of the agency determines by a recorded vote that agency business requires that such meeting be called at an earlier date, in which case the agency shall make public announcement of the time, place, and subject matter of such meeting, and whether open or closed to the public, at the earliest practicable time.

(2) The time or place of a meeting may be changed following the public announcement required by paragraph (1) only if the agency publicly announces such change at the earliest practicable time. The subject matter of a meeting, or the determination of the agency to open or close a meeting, or portion of a meeting, to the public, may be changed following the public announcement required by this subsection only if (A) a majority of the entire membership of the agency determines by a recorded vote that agency business so requires and that no earlier announcement of the change was possible, and (B) the agency publicly announces such change and the vote of each member upon such change at the earliest practicable time.

(3) Immediately following each public announcement required by this subsection, notice of the time, place, and subject matter of a meeting, whether the meeting is open or closed, any change in one of the preceding, and the name and phone number of the official designated by the agency to respond to requests for information about the meeting, shall also be submitted for publication in the Federal Register.

(f)(1) For every meeting closed pursuant to paragraphs (1) through (10) of subsection (c), the General Counsel or chief legal officer of the agency shall publicly certify that, in his or her opinion, the meeting may be closed to the public and shall state each relevant exemptive provision. A copy of such certification, together with a statement from the presiding officer of the meeting setting forth the time and place of the meeting, and the persons present, shall be retained by the agency. The agency shall maintain a complete transcript or electronic recording adequate to record fully the proceedings of each meeting, or portion of a meeting, closed to the public, except that in the case of a meeting, or portion of a meeting, closed to the public pursuant to paragraph (8), (9)(A), or (10) of subsection (c), the agency shall maintain either such a transcript or recording, or a set of minutes. Such minutes shall fully and clearly describe all matters discussed and shall provide a full and accurate summary of any actions taken, and the reasons therefor, including a description of each of the views expressed on any item and the record of any rollcall vote (reflecting the vote of each member on the question). All documents considered in connection with any action shall be identified in such minutes.

(2) The agency shall make promptly available to the public, in a place easily accessible to the public, the transcript, electronic recording, or minutes (as required by paragraph (1)) of the discussion of any item on the agenda, or of any item of the testimony of any witness received at the meeting, except for such item or items of such discussion or testimony as the agency determines

to contain information which may be withheld under subsection (c). Copies of such transcript, or minutes, or a transcription of such recording disclosing the identity of each speaker, shall be furnished to any person at the actual cost of duplication or transcription. The agency shall maintain a complete verbatim copy of the transcript, a complete copy of the minutes, or a complete electronic recording of each meeting, or portion of a meeting, closed to the public, for a period of at least two years after such meeting, or until one year after the conclusion of any agency proceeding with respect to which the meeting or portion was held, whichever occurs later.

(g) Each agency subject to the requirements of this section shall, within 180 days after the date of enactment of this section, following consultation with the Office of the Chairman of the Administrative Conference of the United States and published notice in the Federal Register of at least thirty days and opportunity for written comment by any person, promulgate regulations to implement the requirements of subsections (b) through (f) of this section. Any person may bring a proceeding in the United States District Court for the District of Columbia to require an agency to promulgate such regulations if such agency has not promulgated such regulations within the time period specified herein. Subject to any limitations of time provided by law, any person may bring a proceeding in the United States Court of Appeals for the District of Columbia to set aside agency regulations issued pursuant to this subsection that are not in accord with the requirements of subsections (b) through (f) of this section and to require the promulgation of regulations that are in accord with such subsections.

(h)(1) The district courts of the United States shall have jurisdiction to enforce the requirements of subsections (b) through (f) of this section by declaratory judgment, injunctive relief, or other relief as may be appropriate. Such actions may be brought by any person against an agency prior to, or within sixty days after, the meeting out of which the violation of this section arises, except that if public announcement of such meeting is not initially provided by the agency in accordance with the requirements of this section, such action may be instituted pursuant to this section at any time prior to sixty days after any public announcement of such meeting. Such actions may be brought in the district court of the United States for the district in which the agency meeting is held or in which the agency in question has its headquarters, or in the District Court for the District of Columbia. In such actions a defendant shall serve his answer within thirty days after the service of the complaint. The burden is on the defendant to sustain his action. In deciding such cases the court may examine in camera any portion of the transcript, electronic recording, or minutes of a meeting closed to the public, and may take such additional evidence as it deems necessary. The court, having due regard for orderly administration and the public interest, as well as the interests of the parties, may grant such equitable relief as it deems appropriate, including granting an injunction against future violations of this section or ordering the agency to make available to the public such portion of the transcript, recording, or minutes of a meeting as is not authorized to be withheld under subsection (c) of this section.

(2) Any Federal court otherwise authorized by law to review agency action may, at the application of any person properly participating in the proceeding pursuant to other applicable law, inquire into violations by the agency of the requirements of this section and afford such relief as it deems appropriate. Nothing in this section authorizes any Federal court having jurisdiction solely on the basis of paragraph (1) to set aside, enjoin, or invalidate any agency action (other than an action to close a meeting or to withhold information under this section) taken or discussed at any agency meeting out of which the violation of this section arose.

(i) The court may assess against any party reasonable attorney fees and other litigation costs reasonably incurred by any other party who substantially prevails in any action brought in accordance with the provisions of subsection (g) or (h) of this section, except that costs may be assessed against the plaintiff only where the court finds that the suit was initiated by the plaintiff primarily for frivolous or dilatory purposes. In the case of assessment of costs against an agency, the costs may be assessed by the court against the United States.

(j) Each agency subject to the requirements of this section shall annually report to the Congress regarding the following:

(1) The changes in the policies and procedures of the agency under this section that have occurred during the preceding 1-year period.

(2) A tabulation of the number of meetings held, the exemptions applied to close meetings, and the days of public notice provided to close meetings.

(3) A brief description of litigation or formal complaints concerning the implementation of this section by the agency.

(4) A brief explanation of any changes in law that have affected the responsibilities of the agency under this section.

(k) Nothing herein expands or limits the present rights of any person under section 552 of this title, except that the exemptions set forth in subsection (c) of this section shall govern in the case of any request made pursuant to section 552 to copy or inspect the transcripts, recordings, or minutes described in subsection (f) of this section. The requirements of chapter 33 of title 44, United States Code, shall not apply to the transcripts, recordings, and minutes described in subsection (f) of this section.

(*l*) This section does not constitute authority to withhold any information from Congress, and does not authorize the closing of any agency meeting or portion thereof required by any other provision of law to be open.

(m) Nothing in this section authorizes any agency to withhold from any individual any record, including transcripts, recordings, or minutes required by this section, which is otherwise accessible to such individual under section 552a of this title.

§ 553. Rule making

(a) This section applies, according to the provisions thereof, except to the extent that there is involved —

(1) a military or foreign affairs function of the United States; or

(2) a matter relating to agency management or personnel or to public property, loans, grants, benefits, or contracts.

(b) General notice of proposed rule making shall be published in the Federal Register, unless persons subject thereto are named and either personally served or otherwise have actual notice thereof in accordance with law. The notice shall include —

(1) a statement of the time, place, and nature of public rule making proceedings;

(2) reference to the legal authority under which the rule is proposed; and

(3) either the terms or substance of the proposed rule or a description of the subjects and issues involved. Except when notice or hearing is required by statute, this subsection does not apply —

(A) to interpretative rules, general statements of policy, or rules of agency organization, procedure, or practice; or

(B) when the agency for good cause finds (and incorporates the finding and a brief statement of reasons therefore in the rules issued) that notice and public procedure thereon are impracticable, unnecessary, or contrary to the public interest.

(c) After notice required by this section, the agency shall give interested persons an opportunity to participate in the rule making through submission of written data, views, or arguments with or without opportunity for oral presentation. After consideration of the relevant matter presented, the agency shall incorporate in the rules adopted a concise general statement of their basis and purpose. When rules are required by statute to be made on the record after opportunity for an agency hearing, sections 556 and 557 of this title apply instead of this subsection.

(d) The required publication or service of a substantive rule shall be made not less than 30 days before its effective date, except —

> (1) a substantive rule which grants or recognizes an exemption or relieves a restriction;

> (2) interpretative rules and statements of policy; or

> (3) as otherwise provided by the agency for good cause found and published with the rule.

(e) Each agency shall give an interested person the right to petition for the issuance, amendment, or repeal of a rule.

§ 554. Adjudications

(a) This section applies, according to the provisions thereof, in every case of adjudication required by statute to be determined on the record after opportunity for an agency hearing, except to the extent that there is involved —

> (1) a matter subject to a subsequent trial of the law and the facts de novo in a court;

> (2) the selection or tenure of an employee, except a [4] administrative law judge appointed under section 3105 of this title;

> (3) proceedings in which decisions rest solely on inspections, tests, or elections;

> (4) the conduct of military or foreign affairs functions;

> (5) cases in which an agency is acting as an agent for a court; or

> (6) the certification of worker representatives.

(b) Persons entitled to notice of an agency hearing shall be timely informed of —

> (1) the time, place, and nature of the hearing;

> (2) the legal authority and jurisdiction under which the hearing is to be held; and

> (3) the matters of fact and law asserted.

> When private persons are the moving parties, other parties to the proceeding shall give prompt notice of issues controverted in fact or law; and in other instances agencies may by rule require responsive pleading. In fixing the time and

---

4. So in original.

place for hearings, due regard shall be had for the convenience and necessity of the parties or their representatives.

(c) The agency shall give all interested parties opportunity for —

(1) the submission and consideration of facts, arguments, offers of settlement, or proposals of adjustment when time, the nature of the proceeding, and the public interest permit; and

(2) to the extent that the parties are unable so to determine a controversy by consent, hearing and decision on notice and in accordance with sections 556 and 557 of this title.

(d) The employee who presides at the reception of evidence pursuant to section 556 of this title shall make the recommended decision or initial decision required by section 557 of this title, unless he becomes unavailable to the agency. Except to the extent required for the disposition of ex parte matters as authorized by law, such an employee may not —

(1) consult a person or party on a fact in issue, unless on notice and opportunity for all parties to participate; or

(2) be responsible to or subject to the supervision or direction of an employee or agent engaged in the performance of investigative or prosecuting functions for an agency.

An employee or agent engaged in the performance of investigative or prosecuting functions for an agency in a case may not, in that or a factually related case, participate or advise in the decision, recommended decision, or agency review pursuant to section 557 of this title, except as witness or counsel in public proceedings. This subsection does not apply —

(A) in determining applications for initial licenses;

(B) to proceedings involving the validity or application of rates, facilities, or practices of public utilities or carriers; or

(C) to the agency or a member or members of the body comprising the agency.

(e) The agency, with like effect as in the case of other orders, and in its sound discretion, may issue a declaratory order to terminate a controversy or remove uncertainty.

§ 555. Ancillary matters

(a) This section applies, according to the provisions thereof, except as otherwise provided by this subchapter.

(b) A person compelled to appear in person before an agency or representative thereof is entitled to be accompanied, represented, and advised by counsel or, if permitted by the agency, by other qualified representative. A party is entitled to appear in person or by or with counsel or other duly qualified representative in an agency proceeding. So far as the orderly conduct of public business permits, an interested person may appear before an agency or its responsible employees for the presentation, adjustment, or determination of an issue, request, or controversy in a proceeding, whether interlocutory, summary, or otherwise, or in connection with an agency function. With due regard for the convenience and necessity of the parties or their representatives and within a reasonable time, each agency shall proceed to conclude a matter presented to it. This subsection does not grant or deny a person who is not a lawyer the right to appear for or represent others before an agency or in an agency proceeding.

(c) Process, requirement of a report, inspection, or other investigative act or demand may not be issued, made, or enforced except as authorized by law. A person compelled to submit data or evidence is entitled to retain or, on payment of lawfully prescribed costs, procure a copy or transcript thereof, except that in a nonpublic investigatory proceeding the witness may for good cause be limited to inspection of the official transcript of his testimony.

(d) Agency subpoenas authorized by law shall be issued to a party on request and, when required by rules of procedure, on a statement or showing of general relevance and reasonable scope of the evidence sought. On contest, the court shall sustain the subpoena or similar process or demand to the extent that it is found to be in accordance with law. In a proceeding for enforcement, the court shall issue an order requiring the appearance of the witness or the production of the evidence or data within a reasonable time under penalty of punishment for contempt in case of contumacious failure to comply.

(e) Prompt notice shall be given of the denial in whole or in part of a written application, petition, or other request of an interested person made in connection with any agency proceeding. Except in affirming a prior denial or when the denial is self-explanatory, the notice shall be accompanied by a brief statement of the grounds for denial.

§ 556. Hearings; presiding employees; powers and duties; burden of proof; evidence; record as basis of decision

(a) This section applies, according to the provisions thereof, to hearings required by section 553 or 554 of this title to be conducted in accordance with this section.

(b) There shall preside at the taking of evidence —

(1) the agency;

(2) one or more members of the body which comprises the agency; or

(3) one or more administrative law judges appointed under section 3105 of this title.

This subchapter does not supersede the conduct of specified classes of proceedings, in whole or in part, by or before boards or other employees specially provided for by or designated under statute. The functions of presiding employees and of employees participating in decisions in accordance with section 557 of this title shall be conducted in an impartial manner. A presiding or participating employee may at any time disqualify himself. On the filing in good faith of a timely and sufficient affidavit of personal bias or other disqualification of a presiding or participating employee, the agency shall determine the matter as a part of the record and decision in the case.

(c) Subject to published rules of the agency and within its powers, employees presiding at hearings may —

(1) administer oaths and affirmations;

(2) issue subpoenas authorized by law;

(3) rule on offers of proof and receive relevant evidence;

(4) take depositions or have depositions taken when the ends of justice would be served;

(5) regulate the course of the hearing;

(6) hold conferences for the settlement or simplification of the issues by consent of the parties or by the use of alternative means of dispute resolution as provided in subchapter IV of this chapter;

(7) inform the parties as to the availability of one or more alternative means of dispute resolution, and encourage use of such methods;

(8) require the attendance at any conference held pursuant to paragraph (6) of at least one representative of each party who has authority to negotiate concerning resolution of issues in controversy;

(9) dispose of procedural requests or similar matters;

(10) make or recommend decisions in accordance with section 557 of this title; and

(11) take other action authorized by agency rule consistent with this subchapter.

(d) Except as otherwise provided by statute, the proponent of a rule or order has the burden of proof. Any oral or documentary evidence may be received, but the agency as a matter of policy shall provide for the exclusion of irrelevant, immaterial, or unduly repetitious evidence. A sanction may not be imposed or rule or order issued except on consideration of the whole record or those parts thereof cited by a party and supported by and in accordance with the reliable, probative, and substantial evidence. The agency may, to the extent consistent with the interests of justice and the policy of the underlying statutes administered by the agency, consider a violation of section 557(d) of this title sufficient grounds for a decision adverse to a party who has knowingly committed such violation or knowingly caused such violation to occur. A party is entitled to present his case or defense by oral or documentary evidence, to submit rebuttal evidence, and to conduct such cross-examination as may be required for a full and true disclosure of the facts. In rule making or determining claims for money or benefits or applications for initial licenses an agency may, when a party will not be prejudiced thereby, adopt procedures for the submission of all or part of the evidence in written form.

(e) The transcript of testimony and exhibits, together with all papers and requests filed in the proceeding, constitutes the exclusive record for decision in accordance with section 557 of this title and, on payment of lawfully prescribed costs, shall be made available to the parties. When an agency decision rests on official notice of a material fact not appearing in the evidence in the record, a party is entitled, on timely request, to an opportunity to show the contrary.

§ 557. Initial decisions; conclusiveness; review by agency; submissions by parties; contents of decisions; record

(a) This section applies, according to the provisions thereof, when a hearing is required to be conducted in accordance with section 556 of this title.

(b) When the agency did not preside at the reception of the evidence, the presiding employee or, in cases not subject to section 554(d) of this title, an employee qualified to preside at hearings pursuant to section 556 of this title, shall initially decide the case unless the agency requires, either in specific cases or by general rule, the entire record to be certified to it for decision. When the presiding employee makes an initial decision, that decision then becomes the decision of the agency without further proceedings unless there is an appeal to, or review on motion of, the agency within time provided by rule. On appeal from or review of the initial decision, the agency has all the powers which it would have in making the initial decision except as it may limit the issues on notice or by rule. When the agency makes the decision without having presided at the reception of the evidence, the presiding employee or an employee qualified to preside at hearings pursuant to section 556 of this title shall first recommend a decision, except that in rule making or determining applications for initial licenses —

(1) instead thereof the agency may issue a tentative decision or one of its responsible employees may recommend a decision; or

(2) this procedure may be omitted in a case in which the agency finds on the record that due and timely execution of its functions imperatively and unavoidably so requires.

(c) Before a recommended, initial, or tentative decision, or a decision on agency review of the decision of subordinate employees, the parties are entitled to a reasonable opportunity to submit for the consideration of the employees participating in the decisions —

(1) proposed findings and conclusions; or

(2) exceptions to the decisions or recommended decisions of subordinate employees or to tentative agency decisions; and

(3) supporting reasons for the exceptions or proposed findings or conclusions.

The record shall show the ruling on each finding, conclusion, or exception presented. All decisions, including initial, recommended, and tentative decisions, are a part of the record and shall include a statement of —

(A) findings and conclusions, and the reasons or basis therefore, on all the material issues of fact, law, or discretion presented on the record; and

(B) the appropriate rule, order, sanction, relief, or denial thereof.

(d)(1) In any agency proceeding which is subject to subsection (a) of this section, except to the extent required for the disposition of ex parte matters as authorized by law —

(A) no interested person outside the agency shall make or knowingly cause to be made to any member of the body comprising the agency, administrative law judge, or other employee who is or may reasonably be expected to be involved in the decisional process of the proceeding, an ex parte communication relevant to the merits of the proceeding;

(B) no member of the body comprising the agency, administrative law judge, or other employee who is or may reasonably be expected to be involved in the decisional process of the proceeding, shall make or knowingly cause to be made to any interested person outside the agency an ex parte communication relevant to the merits of the proceeding;

(C) a member of the body comprising the agency, administrative law judge, or other employee who is or may reasonably be expected to be involved in the decisional process of such proceeding who receives, or who makes or knowingly causes to be made, a communication prohibited by this subsection shall place on the public record of the proceeding:

(i) all such written communications;

(ii) memoranda stating the substance of all such oral communications; and

(iii) all written responses, and memoranda stating the substance of all oral responses, to the materials described in clauses (i) and (ii) of this subparagraph;

(D) upon receipt of a communication knowingly made or knowingly caused to be made by a party in violation of this subsection, the agency, administrative law judge, or other employee presiding at the hearing may, to the extent consistent with the interests of justice and the policy of the underlying statutes, require the party to show cause why his claim or interest in the proceeding should not be dismissed, denied, disregarded, or otherwise adversely affected on account of such violation; and

(E) the prohibitions of this subsection shall apply beginning at such time as the agency may designate, but in no case shall they begin to apply later than the time at which a proceeding is noticed for hearing unless the person responsible for the communication has knowledge that it will be noticed, in which case the prohibitions shall apply beginning at the time of his acquisition of such knowledge.

(2) This subsection does not constitute authority to withhold information from Congress.

§ 558. Imposition of sanctions; determination of applications for licenses; suspension, revocation, and expiration of licenses

(a) This section applies, according to the provisions thereof, to the exercise of a power or authority.

(b) A sanction may not be imposed or a substantive rule or order issued except within jurisdiction delegated to the agency and as authorized by law.

(c) When application is made for a license required by law, the agency, with due regard for the rights and privileges of all the interested parties or adversely affected persons and within a reasonable time, shall set and complete proceedings required to be conducted in accordance with sections 556 and 557 of this title or other proceedings required by law and shall make its decision. Except in cases of willfulness or those in which public health, interest, or safety requires otherwise, the withdrawal, suspension, revocation, or annulment of a license is lawful only if, before the institution of agency proceedings therefore, the licensee has been given —

(1) notice by the agency in writing of the facts or conduct which may warrant the action; and

(2) opportunity to demonstrate or achieve compliance with all lawful requirements.

When the licensee has made timely and sufficient application for a renewal or a new license in accordance with agency rules, a license with reference to an activity of a continuing nature does not expire until the application has been finally determined by the agency.

§ 559. Effect on other laws; effect of subsequent statute

This subchapter, chapter 7, and sections 1305, 3105, 3344, 4301(2)(E), 5372, and 7521 of this title, and the provisions of section 5335(a)(B) of this title that relate to administrative law judges, do not limit or repeal additional requirements imposed by statute or otherwise recognized by law. Except as otherwise required by law, requirements or privileges relating to evidence or procedure apply equally to agencies and persons. Each agency is granted the authority necessary to comply with the requirements of this subchapter through the issuance of rules or otherwise. Subsequent statute may not be held to supersede or modify this subchapter, chapter 7, sections 1305, 3105, 3344, 4301(2)(E), 5372, or 7521 of this title, or the provisions of section 5335(a)(B) of this title that relate to administrative law judges, except to the extent that it does so expressly.

Appendix B

Request for Prehearing Order

[Caption]

Respondent Joe Smith's Application for Prehearing Orders

On November 10, 2010, the State Racing Commission gave written notice to the Respondent, Joe Smith, that it intended to take action with respect to the breeding license issued to the Respondent. On November 20, 2010, the Respondent requested an evidentiary hearing, under the provisions of the State Administrative Procedure Act (State APA). The Commission then appointed an Administrative Law Judge to preside over an evidentiary hearing and prepare a report and recommendation to the Commission. The matter has not yet been set for hearing.

The Respondent has a protected property interest in retaining his breeding license. Under State APA section 12.123, this license may be revoked or suspended only after the agency affords the Respondent an opportunity for hearing. Under the Due Process Clause of the Fifth Amendment, the Respondent is entitled to a meaningful opportunity to be heard before the Commission takes any final action with respect to his breeding license. *See Goldberg v. Kelly*, 397 U.S. 254 (1970). The Respondent has a legitimate interest in retaining his breeding license, and while recognizing the Commission's interest in the proper enforcement of its regulations, the Commission has a duty to conduct these proceedings in a manner that will reduce the risk of an erroneous termination of the Respondent's license. *See Mathews v. Eldridge*, 424 U.S. 319 (1976).

To ensure the Respondent has a meaningful opportunity to be heard, the Respondent respectfully requests the following procedural orders:

1. That the Commission be required to provide a more definite statement of the factual premises and allegations supporting the Commission's charges. In particular, the Commission should be directed to disclose (1) a description of the acts which the Commission contends constitutes a violation of law; (2) the date of each action relied upon by the Commission; (3) the location of each action; and (4) a reference to the section of statute or regulation which the Commission claims has been violated based on this action.

2. That the matter be set for a hearing at a date mutually agreed upon by the parties and the ALJ, on a date that is not sooner than 60 days nor later than 120 days from the date of the ALJ's scheduling order.

3. That the ALJ require the parties to exchange copies of any exhibit to be used during the hearing along with the names, addresses, and phone numbers of each witness to be presented at the hearing, and that such exchange take place two weeks before the start of the hearing.

4. That the ALJ certify that she has participated in neither an investigative nor prosecutorial role in this matter. *See Withrow v. Larkin*, 421 U.S. 35 (1975).

Respectfully submitted by:

[counsel for the Respondent]

Certificate of Service

Appendix C

Prehearing Order (where the agency has subpoena authority)

[Caption]

Authority and Jurisdiction

By order of the State Racing Commission and as set forth more completely in its notice to the Respondent Joe Smith, dated June 29, 2010, the State Racing Commission advised Respondent of action it was taking with respect to Respondent's license as a Racing Horse Breeder, and of Respondent's right to a hearing pursuant to the provisions of State Racing Statute [xx-xxx] and State Administrative Procedure Act Chapter [xxx]. Thereafter, the Commission appointed the undersigned to serve as its Administrative Law Judge.

Contact Information

The parties are therefore advised each may contact the Administrative Law Judge at the following address:

[Name of ALJ]

Administrative Law Judge

State Racing Commission

Downtown, State 55005

Note that in the event any party wishes to contact the Administrative Law Judge to discuss a substantive matter, the contact (if in person, by email, or by telephone) shall only take place with all parties participating.

Hearing Location and Time

The evidentiary hearing requested by the Respondent will commence on Friday, November 14, 2010, at 9:00 a.m., at the hearing room of the State Racing Commission or at a room to be designated by the Commission, in Downtown, State, and shall continue from day to day until completed.

Controlling Authority

These proceedings are to be conducted pursuant to the provisions of the State Racing Authority Act (Chapter xx State Revised Code) and the State Administrative Procedure Act (Chapter xx State Revised Code). A copy of the administrative rules controlling these proceedings is available upon request at the Commission office. In the event of any conflict between the provisions of the Commission's statutes and regulations, and any term found in this entry and order, the provisions of the Commission's statutes and regulations shall control.

Filing Requirements

An original of any document required to be filed by the rules applicable to these proceedings shall be filed with the Commission, with simultaneous service of a copy upon the opposing party and, with exceptions as noted below, with the Administrative Law Judge. All motions and briefs shall contain a certificate of service indicating the date and manner that a copy of the document was served on the opposing party, as well as the name, address, and telephone number of the person submitting the motion or brief, and shall be appropriately captioned to indicate the name of the respondent.

Subpoenas

Upon written request of either party, the Commission shall issue subpoenas to compel the attendance and testimony of witnesses and production of books, records and papers at the administrative hearing. Each subpoena shall indicate on whose behalf the witness is required to testify. Copies of such subpoena request shall be mailed to the opposing party or representatives using the address information shown above. Each subpoena request shall specify the name and address of the individual to be served and the date, time, and location at which they are to appear at the administrative hearing. In each case, the subpoena should instruct that the witness is to appear at the beginning of the scheduled hearing, with directions to call in advance of the hearing to confirm the exact time for appearing at the hearing. If the subpoena includes a duces tecum request, the specific documents or tangible things to be produced at the administrative hearing shall be listed in the request. Any party needing subpoenas or subpoenas duces tecum shall file the request for these subpoenas so the request is received by the Commission no later than 4:00 p.m. on the 30th day before the date set for the start of this hearing.

Upon motion filed not later than five days after a request for subpoena has been filed, and for good cause shown, the Commission or its Administrative Law Judge may order any subpoena be quashed. The non-moving party may file a response no later than three days after service of the motion to quash or at least one day prior to the date of compliance, whichever is earlier, and either party may request oral argument on the merits of the motion, but absent such a request, oral argument will be deemed waived. In the event that the number of subpoenas requested appears to be unreasonable, the Commission's Administrative Law Judge may require a showing of necessity therefor, and, in the absence of such showing, may limit the number of subpoenas. Absent such a limitation and in the absence of the timely filing of a motion to quash, subpoenas shall be issued within five days of the Commission's receipt of each properly prepared subpoena request. In the absence of a timely filed motion to quash, the Commission's failure to issue subpoenas within this time may constitute sufficient grounds for the granting of a continuance. Unless a motion to quash has been granted, a witness shall attend the hearing to which he or she was subpoenaed. The Commission shall make a reasonable attempt to contact any witness whose subpoena was served on the witness and was thereafter quashed. Witnesses may not be subpoenaed to prehearing conferences.

Depositions In Lieu of Appearance

Upon written motion of any representative of record, and upon service of that motion to all other representatives, the Administrative Law Judge may order that the testimony of a witness be taken by deposition in lieu of testimony during the scheduled hearing, and that any designated books, papers, documents or tangible objects, not privileged, be produced at the same time and place if it appears probable that:

(1) The witness will be unavailable to attend or will be prevented from attending a hearing;

(2) The testimony of the witness is material; and

(3) The testimony of the witness is necessary in order to prevent a failure of justice.

Note that in the case of an expert witness, a showing of the unavailability of the expert shall not be necessary for the Administrative Law Judge's consideration of the motion of a representative to take a deposition in lieu of testimony during the scheduled hearing.

The representatives shall agree to the time and place for taking the deposition in lieu of testimony during the scheduled hearing, and shall arrange for the depositions to be completed by no later than ten days after the start of the scheduled hearing. Depositions shall be conducted in the same county in which the hearing is conducted unless otherwise agreed to by the representatives. If the representatives are unable to agree, the Administrative Law Judge shall set the time and fix the place of deposition. At a deposition taken pursuant to this order, representatives shall have the right, as at hearing, to fully examine witnesses. The Administrative Law Judge has the discretion to be present at such a deposition. A transcript of any deposition taken under this order shall be filed with the Commission within twenty-one days of the date the deposition was concluded, and shall be offered into evidence at hearing by the representative requesting the deposition, in lieu of the witness's testimony at hearing, and may also be offered by the party responding to the request for the preservation of such testimony. The cost of preparing a transcript of any testimony taken by deposition in lieu of live testimony shall be borne by the Commission. In the event of appeal, such costs shall be made a part of the cost of the hearing record. The expense of any video deposition shall be borne by the requestor. Any deposition or transcript of prior testimony of a witness may be used for the purpose of refreshing the recollection, contradicting the testimony, or impeaching the credibility of that witness. If only a part of a deposition or transcript of prior testimony is offered into evidence by a representative, the opposing representative may offer any other part. Nothing in this order shall be construed to permit the taking of depositions for purposes other than for use at the evidentiary hearing now scheduled in this matter. A transcript of testimony and exhibits from a prior proceeding may be introduced for any purpose if that prior proceeding forms the basis for the allegations in the current case. Upon offering part of a transcript or exhibit from deposition in lieu of appearance or from a prior proceeding, the offering representative shall make the entire transcript available at least one week before the scheduled start of the hearing.

Motions

Any party seeking to present motions in limine or other prehearing motions shall do so no later than thirty days prior to the scheduled start of the hearing. All motions, unless made upon the record at the hearing, shall be made in writing. A written motion shall state with particularity the relief or order sought, shall be accompanied by a memorandum setting forth the grounds therefor, and shall be filed with the Commission, with copies to all opposing parties and to the Administrative Law Judge. Within seven days after service of a written prehearing motion, a response to that motion may be filed. A movant may reply to a response only with the permission of the Administrative Law Judge.

Prehearing Exchanges

The parties shall mark each exhibit they intend to introduce at the hearing (with the State using numbers and the Respondent using letters). At the time of the hearing, the party intending to introduce an exhibit shall present the original (or certified copy) plus one copy for the Administrative Law Judge. On or before 4:00 p.m. on the fourteenth day before the hearing, the parties shall exchange information providing the name, address, and phone numbers of each witness the party intends to call as a witness, and shall identify each document intended to be introduced at hearing. A notice disclosing the name of each witness and a brief summary of each document shall be filed with the Commission contemporaneously with the exchange. Failure without good cause to comply with this direction may result in exclusion from the hearing of such testimony or documents, upon motion of the representative to whom disclosure is refused. The parties are further directed to prepare and exchange with each other copies of the exhibits each intends to introduce at the hearing. These copies are to be exchanged no later than fourteen days before the scheduled start of the hearing, with service considered effective upon mailing.

Where the party intends to present an exhibit that is not a document, the exhibit shall be made available for inspection by adverse counsel no later than fourteen days before the scheduled start of the hearing.

Copies of the exhibits are not to be served upon either the Commission or the Administrative Law Judge in advance of the hearing, but both parties shall file with the Commission a notice identifying the exhibits presented and a list of witnesses the party intends to call. Any written report prepared by an expert for use during the evidentiary hearing must be exchanged no later than fourteen days before the scheduled start of the hearing. Any written report by an expert required to be exchanged under this order shall set forth the opinions to which the expert will testify and the bases for such opinions. The failure of a party to produce a written report from an expert fully conforming to the terms of this order may for good cause shown result in the exclusion of that expert's testimony at hearing.

The failure of a party to produce an exhibit under the terms of this order may result in the exclusion of that exhibit from evidence. The failure of a party to identify a lay or expert witness under the terms of this order may result in the exclusion of that witness's testimony at the hearing.

Continuances and Counsel

The evidentiary hearing now scheduled to begin on November 14, 2010, shall not be delayed upon motion by a representative unless a showing of reasonable cause and proper diligence is presented. Before granting any continuance or delay, consideration shall be given to harm to the public that may result from delay in proceedings. In no event will a motion for a continuance by a representative, requested less than seven days prior to the scheduled date of the hearing, be granted unless it is demonstrated that an extraordinary situation exists which could not have been anticipated and which would justify the granting of a continuance. The Respondent currently is representing himself, without an attorney. The statutes controlling these proceedings permit an individual to represent himself or herself without counsel, but also permit respondents to appear through an attorney licensed to practice law in State. The Respondent is advised that undue delay in securing the services of an attorney will not constitute good cause to delay the evidentiary hearing in this matter, and is advised to seek the timely advice of an attorney in advance of the hearing.

There will be a final prehearing telephone conference on November 7, 2010, at 12:15 p.m. The purpose of this conference will be to confirm the need for an evidentiary hearing, explain the hearing procedures, and resolve any remaining prehearing issues raised by the parties' motions. The Administrative Law Judge will initiate the call, using the telephone numbers provided by the parties.

Either party may request a clarification or correction of this entry, by no later than ten days from the date of mailing, as shown below.

Restatement of Schedule

1. [date ten days from date of mailing of this prehearing order]: request for clarification or correction of this prehearing entry;

2. [date 30 days before the scheduled hearing date]: requests for subpoenas and subpoenas duces tecum must be received by the Commission;

3. [date 14 days before the scheduled hearing date]: exchange of witness list and copies of all exhibits; exchange of expert reports;

4. [date seven days before the scheduled hearing date]: final prehearing telephone conference at 12:15 p.m.

5. [hearing date], and continuing thereafter: evidentiary hearing on all matters not resolved through any motions in limine.

It is so ordered.

[signature and certificate of mailing]

APPENDIX D

PREHEARING ORDER ALTERNATIVE
(NO APA AND NO SUBPOENA AUTHORITY)

Journal Entry and Notice of Hearing

The Petitioner in this proceeding is the city of Downtown, State; and the Respondents in this proceeding are three Downtown employees, who worked at the city's Real Estate Division. These are proceedings taken pursuant to the provisions of State Retirement Code 45-1-11 (appeal of staff determination), in which the Petitioner challenges a senior staff determination by the State Public Employees Retirement System (SPERS), which held the Respondents' service with the City rendered them eligible for membership in the System. Upon its receipt of the Petitioner's request for administrative review and after the appointment of an Administrative Law Judge, the parties met by telephone conference on July 24, 2011, with appearances as shown above.

Date of Hearing

By agreement of the parties, the evidentiary hearing in this matter is scheduled to begin on Wednesday, September 26, 2011, at 9:00 a.m. in the System's office, located at 2 East Street in Downtown, State, with notice of room designation to follow.

Status of the Case

These proceedings are controlled by the provisions of section 45-1-11 of the State Administrative Code, controlling appeals of determinations made by staff of the System. Section 45-1-11(C)(1)(a) requires that the Administrative Law Judge conduct a hearing and issue a report and recommendation to the System's trustees. That is the purpose of the proceeding that is now scheduled for September 26, 2011. Further, at the time evidence is taken, there will be a record made, pursuant to Section 45-1-11(C)(1)(b). That section also provides that "parties to the appeal and staff are permitted to submit evidence in the form of witness testimony and any form of documentation." Accordingly, the parties should anticipate a hearing process by which traditional forms of adversarial adjudication take place, using tools like those available to the parties in a civil trial. If a party seeks to have evidence presented for consideration by the System or its ALJ, it must offer the evidence, and it must do so in a way that permits an opponent to challenge the offer so that a record can be made of whether the evidence is admissible or not. While the State Rules of Evidence are not applicable, they do serve as a guide to controlling the flow of information permitted into or kept out of the adjudicative process. And while the State Rules of Civil Procedure likewise do not apply, the Rules do offer some guidance as to steps that can be taken to efficiently and fairly develop a record that will be useful to the members of the System or its ALJ when they make the final adjudication order in this matter.

At the outset notice is given that the undersigned is not supervised or controlled by the investigative or prosecutorial sections of the System and has never investigated or prosecuted any matter now pending before the System. Having examined the record to familiarize myself with the nature of the case generally, I find no claim, issue, or premise that would create a conflict of interest with my offering to serve as the System's Administrative Law Judge. Nevertheless, the parties may make known any objection to my serving as the Administrative Law Judge, providing they do so in a timely fashion. Any objection to my service as the ALJ for this matter upon claim of conflict of interest or for any other reason now known by the parties, shall be filed with the System in writing and shall be received by the System not later than 4:00 p.m. on August 10, 2011, or such claim shall be deemed waived.

Burden and Degree of Proof

In this case the City of Downtown—Real Estate Division challenges a determination made by SPERS senior staff finding that the Claimants were eligible for membership in SPERS at a time when the City failed to make required contributions to the System. In order to establish that their service during the period in question meets all of the qualifications for membership in SPERS, the claimants have the affirmative obligation of establishing by a preponderance of the evidence a factual and legal basis for their claim. That burden, however, may be met by the admission into evidence of the SPERS senior staff report announcing the staff's determination that the claimants' claims were approved. Upon receiving into evidence the senior staff report, the burden of proving the claimants' ineligibility for membership in SPERS is with the City of Downtown. Accordingly, the City of Downtown has the burden of proving the merits of its challenge to the senior staff determination, and that burden may be met only by proof upon a preponderance of the evidence. After the City has presented its case, the claimants will be provided an opportunity to rebut any evidence or claim presented by the City. No further evidence will be taken once the claimants have been given the opportunity for rebuttal. Should any party object to the allocation of the burden of proof, or to the requirement that such proof be by a preponderance of the evidence, or to the order of hearing, such objection shall be filed by not later than 4:00 p.m. on August 10, 2011, or shall be deemed waived.

Operational and Procedural Requirements

While neither the Rules of Evidence nor the Rules of Civil Procedure are directly applicable to these proceedings, the hearing must nonetheless be fair, and must meet constitutional minimum thresholds applicable whenever the government is in a position to adversely affect the liberty or property rights of its citizens. Further, the Administrative Law Judge is authorized through the grant of authority in Section 45-1-11(C) to take steps to ensure the efficient and orderly creation of a record for use by the System or its ALJ. In furtherance of those goals, the following prehearing orders are entered:

1.   In order to facilitate the order of the hearing and to avoid undue surprise and waste of time during the hearing, the parties shall exchange lists identifying the witnesses each intends to call, and shall provide a short (one or two sentence) summary of the subject the witness shall testify about. This witness list shall be filed by not later than 4:00 p.m. on September 12, 2011.

2.   In the event the witness is offered as an expert witness and has prepared a report in order to express an opinion as an expert, a copy of that report shall be provided to all counsel of record. This exchange shall be made not later than 4:00 p.m. on September 12, 2011.

3.   Each party shall provide the other parties with a copy of each document the party intends to rely on at the time of the hearing. Prior to exchanging these documents, the parties shall mark each document for use as an exhibit, with the Claimants using their last names and numbers in series, e.g., Claimant Jones's Exhibit 1, and the City's exhibits using letters of the alphabet, e.g., City's Exhibit A. If counsel for SPERS intends to offer exhibits, they shall be marked as SPERS Exhibit A (and successive letters of the alphabet). The parties may also submit joint exhibits, as Joint Exhibit 1 (and successive numbers). These copies shall be delivered so that the receiving party receives the documents by not later than 4:00 p.m. on September 12, 2011. The claimants may, if they so choose, offer agreed-upon exhibits, in which case the exhibit should indicate that it is being submitted on behalf of all claimants (or on behalf of specified claimants).

4.   Unless a party is otherwise instructed, copies of the exhibits are not to be provided to the Administrative Law Judge in advance of the hearing. At the time of the hearing, the party offering the document shall bring the original plus two copies of each proposed exhibit. The party shall offer the original or an appropriately certified copy to be retained by the court reporter until the record is delivered to the System or its ALJ at the close of the hearing; one copy shall be delivered at the start of the hearing to the Administrative Law Judge, and one copy shall be made available for use by witnesses while testifying at the hearing.

5.   Each party shall provide the Administrative Law Judge and all other parties with a copy of the list of witnesses, and a list identifying each document and the corresponding exhibit number or letter. This list of witnesses and exhibits shall be filed with the System or its ALJ by not later than 4:00 p.m. on September 12, 2011.

6.   Unless good cause is shown justifying a contrary result, the parties shall be limited to presenting the documents exchanged in accordance with this order, and shall be limited to presenting the testimony of witnesses identified in this list, in accordance with this order.

7.   Any party may request the appearance of any witness known to have relevant information with respect to these proceedings. In the event a party seeks the appearance of a witness known to be represented by counsel, such request shall be directed to counsel of record with the request that the witness be made available to give sworn testimony on September 26, 2011, setting forth the time and location of the evidentiary hearing. Note that neither the System nor the Administrative Law Judge have the power to compel the presence of a witness through the use of a subpoena. Nevertheless, the requesting party shall be permitted to make a record of the efforts employed to secure the testimony of the witness, and may offer as evidence the witness's refusal to testify where such refusal may be relevant to issues in the proceedings (e.g., as where the witness is an affiant and his or her affidavit is offered as evidence; the circumstances of the witness's refusal to testify with respect to information contained in that affidavit may be considered by the Administrative Law Judge if the affidavit is offered as evidence, when weighing the evidentiary value of the affidavit). All such requests shall be in writing, shall be valid only if the witness is identified by name and if the request is accompanied by sufficient information as to permit the recipient to timely locate the witness; and shall be served upon the witness or the witness's legal representative so as to be received by not later than 4:00 p.m. on August 27, 2011.

8.   Upon written motion of any representative of record, and upon service of that motion to all other representatives, the Administrative Law Judge may order that the testimony of a witness be taken at a time other than the time scheduled for this hearing, if it appears that each of the following conditions exist:

(1) The witness will be unavailable to attend or will be prevented from attending the scheduled hearing;

(2) The testimony of the witness is material; and

(3) The testimony of the witness is necessary in order to prevent a failure of justice.

If the representatives are unable to agree, the Administrative Law Judge shall set the time and fix the place of the taking of the witness's testimony. At such time, the representatives shall have the right, as at hearing, to fully examine the witness. The Administrative Law Judge has the discretion to be present at the taking of such testimony. A transcript of any proceedings taken under this order shall be filed with the System or its ALJ not later than 4:00 p.m. on September 25, 2011, and shall be offered into evidence at hearing by the representative seeking the testimony, in lieu of the witness's testimony at hearing. The cost of preparing a transcript of any testimony taken pursuant to this order shall be borne by the System. The expense of any video recording of such testimony shall be borne by the requestor.

9.   Any deposition or transcript of prior testimony of a witness may be used for the purpose of refreshing the recollection, contradicting the testimony or impeaching the credibility of that witness. If only a part of a deposition of prior testimony is offered into evidence by a representative, upon timely motion made within five days of the date of service of the partial transcript, the opposing representative may move to inspect the entire transcript and thereafter may move to require introduction of any other part.

10. Nothing in this order shall be construed to permit the taking of discovery depositions, nor is discovery under the State Rules of Civil Procedure available to the parties.

11. Nothing in this order prohibits the parties from gaining access to any information made public by the operation of state law. This Administrative Law Judge, however, has no authority to enforce any right or claim made pursuant to any public record law.

12. Any party seeking to present motions in limine or other prehearing motions (other than a motion to delay the proceedings, to challenge the appointment of the ALJ, or to challenge the determination of the allocation of the burden of proof) shall do so by not later than 4:00 p.m. on August 27, 2011. A response to any such motion shall be due within five days of the date the motion is served on the party. The party making the motion may reply to a response only upon application to and with the permission of the Administrative Law Judge.

13. The evidentiary hearing now scheduled to begin on September 26, 2011, shall not be continued upon motion by a representative unless a showing of reasonable cause and proper diligence is presented. Before granting any continuance, consideration shall be given to harm to the public, which may result from delay in proceedings. In no event will a motion for a continuance by a representative, requested less than seven days prior to the scheduled date of the hearing, be granted unless it is demonstrated that an extraordinary situation exists that could not have been anticipated and that would justify the granting of a continuance. The claimants currently are representing his or her own cause, without an attorney. The statutes and regulations controlling these proceedings permit an individual to represent

himself or herself without counsel, but also permit respondents to appear through an attorney licensed to practice law in State. Each claimant is advised that undue delay in securing the services of an attorney will not constitute good cause to delay the evidentiary hearing in this matter, and is encouraged to seek the timely advice of an attorney in advance of the hearing.

14. All briefs, memoranda, motions, or other pleadings are subject to the following requirements:

(a) If any unreported court decision is cited in any brief or memorandum, a copy of such decision is to be attached to the brief or memorandum containing the citation.

(b) All briefs, memoranda, motions, or other pleadings must be filed with SPERS within three days after service. A certificate of service is to be attached attesting both to the service of a copy of the pleading on all parties and the provision of a copy to the Administrative Law Judge. This requirement does not apply to the delivery of documents which are intended to be used as evidence at the hearing; such documents are to be exchanged between the parties in the manner provided for by this order, but in the absence of a specific request by the Administrative Law Judge, documents intended for use during the hearing should not be provided to the Administrative Law Judge until the time the hearing is convened.

(c) Only those pleadings, orders, and other papers filed with SPERS at its office at 277 East Street, Downtown, State, will be a part of the official record.

15. The parties may settle or stipulate to anything presented in this administrative review at any time prior to the SPERS System or its ALJ taking action on the matter. During the course of the evidentiary hearing or any prehearing motions, the participants to the proceeding may enter into oral stipulations of fact, procedure, or the authenticity of documents that will be incorporated into the record and will bind the participants. Oral stipulations are to be reduced to writing and submitted to the Administrative Law Judge.

16. Any party may make objections to the evidentiary and legal rulings made during these proceedings. If the Administrative Law Judge refuses to admit evidence or testimony, the participant seeking admission of same may make a proffer thereof and such proffer will be made a part of the record of the hearing, but will not be considered when the Administrative Law Judge prepares the written report and recommendation for the System or its ALJ.

17. There will be a final prehearing status conference beginning at 11:30 a.m. on Wednesday, September 19, 2011. The purpose of the final prehearing status conference is to determine whether there continues to be a need for an evidentiary

hearing, to address any remaining procedural issues, and to permit the parties to inquire as to the order of hearing.

18. Any party may apply for a clarification of these orders or may seek a further procedural order that will facilitate the efficient and fair presentation of evidence, provided such application is received by the System or its ALJ by not later than 4:00 p.m. on August 10, 2011.

Review of Prehearing Calendar:

1. August 10, 2011: any motions for clarification or correction of this Journal Entry, or objections to this Entry.

2. August 10, 2011: filing of any motions challenging any order with respect to the appointment of the Administrative Law Judge; and the filing of any motions challenging the order with respect to the order of the hearing, with respect to who bears the burden of proof, and with respect to the degree of proof required in these proceedings.

3. August 27, 2011: service of requests seeking the attendance of witnesses at the hearing.

4. September 12, 2011: exchange of documents intended for use during the hearing; exchange of list identifying each witness who will be testifying at the hearing; service of copies of any expert reports; deadline for filing motions in limine.

5. September 19, 2011: final prehearing telephone conference at 11:30 a.m.

6. September 25, 2011: filing with the System of any transcript of testimony taken prior to the evidentiary hearing.

7. September 26, 2011, and continuing from day to day: evidentiary hearing provided for by Section 45-1-11.

It is so ordered.

_____   _____

Date   [name of judge]

                    Administrative Law Judge

State Public Retirement System

CERTIFICATE OF SERVICE

I certify that the original of this document was served upon the State Public Employees Retirement System at its offices in Downtown, State, by U.S. mail posted on July 27, 2011, with instructions to forward time-stamped copies to the parties; and that copies of the same were served on July 27, 2011, by fax transmission, upon those parties who provided the fax numbers shown above.

_____

[Name of Judge], Administrative Law Judge

INDEX

A

ADMINISTRATIVE LAW JUDGES
Central panel concept, 18 to 19
Determining credentials and
employment of fact finder, 17
to 18
Employee or contractor of agency, 18
to 20
Independence and fairness, 18
Judicial independence, 15 to 16
Judicialized vs. institutionalized
hearings, 16 to 17
Marshaling of evidence, duties, 52
Non-central panel proceedings, 19 to 20
Open meetings laws, agency reviews of
ALJ reports, 40 to 41
Prosecutorial role, 4
Role of, generally, 4, 7 to 8

ADMINISTRATIVE NOTICE, 55 to 56

**ADMINISTRATIVE PROCEDURE
ACTS**
Applicability, 11
Federal Administrative Procedure
Act, 73 to 121. (*See* **Federal
Administrative Procedure
Act**)
Model APA, 11
Variations in versions, 13
Role of, generally, 11 to 13
Version applicable, 13

**ADMINISTRATIVE SUBPOENAS, 35,
41 to 43**
Enforcement, 42 to 43
Tactical value, 41 to 42

AFFIDAVIT OF OFFICER
Weight given
Affirmative defense overcoming, 9

AFFIRMATIVE DEFENSES
Burden of proving, 8

Enabling statutes, 9

AGENCY REGULATIONS
Burden of proof to be set out, 8
Challenge of underlying regulation or
statutory authority, 25 to 26
Description of scope of hearing, 8
Reading in conjunction with statutes, 5
Version of APA applicable, 13

AGENDAS
Open meetings laws, 38 to 40

ALJ. (*See* **Administrative law judges**)

**ALTERNATIVE DISPUTE
RESOLUTION**, 67 to 68

ATTORNEYS
Fee awards, 68 to 69
Right to counsel, 4
Federal Administrative Procedure
Act, 115 to 116
Role in inquisitorial hearings, 28 to 29

B

BURDEN OF PROOF
Differences in, 8 to 9, 25
Federal Administrative Procedure Act,
116 to 118
Litigator duty to create clear record, 52

C

CENTRAL PANEL CONCEPT
Administrative law judges, 18 to 19

**CHALLENGE OF UNDERLYING
REGULATION OR
STATUTORY AUTHORITY**, 25
to 26

National Institute for Trial Advocacy

G

GOOD FAITH NEGOTIATIONS, 66

H

HABEAS CORPUS, 63 to 64

HEALTH AND SAFETY
Discovery, 3 to 4

HEARSAY EVIDENCE, 9 to 10, 56

I

IMPLIED CONSENT
Driving under the influence
Illustration of difference between
court trials and agency
hearings, 5 to 8
Which branch of government acting
as fact finder, 17

INDEPENDENCE
Administrative law judges, 15 to 16, 18

IN LIMINE MOTIONS
Evidence, 54 to 55

INQUISITION
Art of, 28
Collaborating with inquisitor, 29
Enforcement inquisitions, 30 to 31
Entitlement inquisitions, limitations,
29 to 30

**INSTRUCTIONS ABOUT AGENCY
PROCESS**, 2, 24

INVESTIGATIVE SUBPOENAS, 3, 41
to 42

J

JUDICIAL INDEPENDENCE
Administrative law judges, 15 to 16

JURISDICTION
Barriers to jurisdiction, 1
Differences based on time, 3

L

LACHES, 3

LAWYERS
Fee awards, 68 to 69
Right to counsel, 4
Federal Administrative Procedure
Act, 115 to 116
Role in inquisitorial hearings, 28 to 29

**LICENSE REVOCATION ACTIONS BY
AGENCIES**
Alcoholic beverage sales
Recognition of relevant government
functions, 23 to 24
Categories of disputes, 2
Dental license, collateral attack analysis
regarding, 60 to 61
Discovery, 3 to 4
Drivers' licenses
Implied consent hearing
Illustration of difference between
court trials and agency
hearings, 5 to 8
Federal Administrative Procedure Act,
120 to 121
Medical license
Open meetings laws, 39
Role of APA, 11 to 13
Statutes of limitation, 3
Subpoenas, 3

LIMITATION OF ACTIONS
Control of hearings, 6
Jurisdictional differences based on time,
3
Lack of, 1

M

MANDAMUS, 61 to 62

MARSHALING OF EVIDENCE, 52

W

**WHY IS AGENCY HEARING THIS
CASE**
Illustration of difference between court
trials and agency hearings
Implied consent hearing, 5 to 7

NOTES

NOTES

NOTES